Lecture Notes of the Institute for Computer Sciences, Social Informatics and Telecommunications Engineering

463

More information about this series at https://link.springer.com/bookseries/8197

Mahdi H. Miraz · Garfield Southall · Maaruf Ali ·
Andrew Ware (Eds.)

Emerging Technologies in Computing

5th EAI International Conference, iCETiC 2022
Chester, UK, August 15–16, 2022
Proceedings

Springer

Editors
Mahdi H. Miraz ⓘ
Xiamen University
Xiamen, Malaysia

Garfield Southall ⓘ
University of Chester
Chester, UK

Maaruf Ali ⓘ
University of the West of Scotland
Scotland, UK

Andrew Ware ⓘ
University of South Wales
Newport, UK

ISSN 1867-8211   ISSN 1867-822X (electronic)
Lecture Notes of the Institute for Computer Sciences, Social Informatics
and Telecommunications Engineering
ISBN 978-3-031-25160-3   ISBN 978-3-031-25161-0 (eBook)
https://doi.org/10.1007/978-3-031-25161-0

This Springer imprint is published by the registered company Springer Nature Switzerland AG
The registered company address is: Gewerbestrasse 11, 6330 Cham, Switzerland

Preface

It is our great pleasure to introduce the proceedings of the Fifth International Conference on Emerging Technologies in Computing (iCETiC 2022), held on the 15th and 16th August, 2022. This year, the conference was physically held at the University of Chester, UK. This was an important move towards the 'old normal' following the COVID-19 pandemic.

The theme of iCETiC 2022 was 'Emerging Technologies' as outlined by the 2021 Gartner Hype Cycle for Emerging Technologies. This conference drew together international researchers and developers from both academia and industry in the domains of computing, networking and communications engineering.

iCETiC 2022 was organised by the International Association for Educators and Researchers (IAER). As a knowledge partner, the European Alliance for Innovation (EAI) also played a significant role, both in organising the conference and publishing the proceedings.

The technical program of iCETiC 2022 consisted of 12 full papers in oral presentation sessions in the main conference tracks. The primary conference tracks were:

- Track 1 – Information and Network Security;
- Track 2 – Cloud, IoT, and Distributed Computing;
- Track 3 – AI, Expert Systems, and Big Data Analytics.

The papers were selected from 54 submissions using a blind review process in which each submission was reviewed by at least 3 Technical Program Committee members.

Apart from the high-quality technical paper presentations, the technical program featured two keynote speeches given by Vic Grout from Wrexham Glyndŵr University, UK, and Jonathan C. Roberts from Bangor University, UK.

It was a great pleasure to work with such an excellent organising committee team, who put in significant effort in organising and supporting the conference. The work of the Technical Programme Committee members is also much appreciated: they completed the peer-review process for the technical papers culminating in a high-quality professional programme.

Yet again, iCETiC 2022 provided an excellent forum for researchers, developers and practitioners to discuss recent advancements in computing, networking and communications engineering. We will continue to strive to ensure that future iCETiC conferences will be as successful and stimulating.

Thank you

August 2022

Mahdi H. Miraz
Garfield Southall
Maaruf Ali
Andrew Ware

Organization

Steering Committee Co-chairs

Garfield Southall	University of Chester, UK
Maaruf Ali	University of the West of Scotland, UK
Andrew Ware	University of South Wales, UK
Mahdi H. Miraz	Xiamen University Malaysia, and Wrexham Glyndwr University, UK

Organizing Committee

General Co-chairs

Garfield Southall	University of Chester, UK
Maaruf Ali	University of the West of Scotland, UK

Advisory Board

Andrew Jones	School of Computer Science, University of Hertfordshire, UK
Yousuf M. Islam	Vice-chancellor, Daffodil International University, Bangladesh

Programme Co-chairs

Andrew Ware	University of South Wales, UK
Mahdi H. Miraz	Xiamen University, Malaysia, and Wrexham Glyndwr University, UK

Web, Publicity, and Social Media Chair

Shayma K. Miraz
Administration Officer, International Association for Educators and Researchers (IAER), London, UK

Publications Chair

Mahdi H. Miraz
Xiamen University, Malaysia, and Wrexham Glyndwr University, UK

Local Chair

Anowarul Karim
Head, Logistic Support, International Association for Educators and Researchers (IAER), London, UK

Technical Program Committee Chair

Mohammad Riyaz Belgaum
Universiti Kuala Lumpur (UniKL), Malaysia

Track Chairs

Cloud, IoT and Distributed Computing Track Chair

Will Serrano
University College London, UK

Software Engineering Track Chair

M. Abdullah-Al-Wadud
Associate Professor, Department of Software Engineering, College of Computer and Information Systems, King Saud University, Saudi Arabia

Communications Engineering and Vehicular Technology Track Chair

Mohab A. Mangoud
Department of Electrical and Electronics Engineering, College of Engineering, University of Bahrain, Bahrain

AI, Expert Systems, and Big Data Analytics Track Chair

Christian Esposito — Dipartimento di Informatica, Università degli Studi di Salerno, Italy

Web Information Systems and Applications Track Chair

Marie Nour Haikel-Elsabeh — Pole Léonard de Vinci, France

Security Track Chair

Bhawani Shankar Chowdhry — Distinguished National Professor and Dean, Faculty of Electrical, Electronics, & Computer Engineering, Mehran University of Engineering and Technology, Pakistan

Database System and Application Track Chair

Abdullah Tansel — The City University of New York (CUNY), USA

Economics and Business Engineering Track Chair

Olga Angelopoulou — Senior Lecturer (Assistant Professor), School of Computer Science, University of Hertfordshire, UK

mLearning and eLearning Track Chair

Sergey Lupin — Dean, International Students Department, National Research University for Electronic Technology (MIET), Russia

General Track Chair

Andrew Jones — School of Computer Science, University of Hertfordshire, UK

Technical Program Committee

Renaud Lambiotte — Associate Professor of Networks and Nonlinear Systems, University of Oxford, UK

Ljiljana Trajkovic — School of Engineering Science, Faculty of Applied Sciences, Simon Fraser University, Canada

Been-Chian Chien — Department of Computer Science and Information Engineering, National University of Tainan, Taiwan

Balakrishnan K.   HoD, Electrical & Electronics Engineering,
                                   Karpaga Vinayaga College of Engineering and
                                   Technology, India
Asadullah Shaikh   Assistant Professor and Head of Research, Najran
                                   University, Saudi Arabia
Ibrahim Kucukkoc   Assistant Professor and Research Fellow,
                                   Balikesir University, Turkey
Cristóvão Dias   Centro de Física Teórica e Computacional,
                                   Faculdade de Ciências da Universidade de
                                   Lisboa, Portugal
Radoslaw Michalski   Faculty of Computer Science and Management,
                                   Wroclaw University of Science and
                                   Technology, Poland
Samina Rajper   Assistant Professor, Department of Computer
                                   Science, Shah Abdul Latif University, Pakistan
Wasan Shakir Awad   Dean, College of Information Technology, Ahlia
                                   University, Bahrain
Prabhat K. Mahanti   Professor, Department of Computer Science,
                                   University of New Brunswick, Canada
Massimo Ficco   Associate Professor, Department of Information
                                   Engineering (DII), Università degli Studi della
                                   Campania Luigi Vanvitelli, Italy
Syed Faiz Ahmed   Universiti Kuala Lumpur, Malaysia
Mohammad Siraj   Assistant Professor, College of Engineering, King
                                   Saud University, Saudi Arabia
José Javier Ramasco   University of the Balearic Islands, Spain
Zi-Ke Zhang   Hangzhou Normal University, China
Francisco Rodrigues   University of São Paulo, Brazil
Ahmed N. Al Masri   Assistant Professor & Director of the Patent
                                   Office, College of Education, American
                                   University in the Emirates, UAE
Ahmed Bin Touq   United Arab Emirates University, UAE
Daniel Onah   University College London, UK
Oussama Hamid   Assistant Professor, Department of Computer
                                   Science, University of Kurdistan Hewlêr, Iraq
Souvik Pal   Assistant Professor, Department of Computer
                                   Science and Engineering, Elitte College of
                                   Engineering, Kolkata, India
Ali Hessami   Vega Systems Ltd, UK
Ezendu Ariwa   Department of Computer Science and
                                   Technology, University of Bedfordshire, UK
Umair Ahmed   Assistant Professor, Gulf University, Bahrain

Aamir Zeb Shaikh   Assistant Professor, Department of Electrical Engineering, NED University of Engineering and Technology, Pakistan

Farhat Naureen Memon   Associate Professor, Institute of Mathematics and Computer Science, University of Sindh, Pakistan

Fida Hussain Chandio   Associate Professor, Institute of Mathematics and Computer Science, University of Sindh, UAE

Riaz Ahmed Shaikh   Assistant Professor, Department of Computer Science, Shah Abdul Latif University, Pakistan

Muniba Memon   Assistant Professor, Department of Computer Science, Najran University, Saudi Arabia

Mansoor Hyder Depar   Director, Information Technology Centre (ITC), Sindh Agriculture University (SAU), Pakistan

Zohreh Dehghani Champiri   Faculty of Computer Science & Information Technology, University of Malaya, Malaysia

Md Tanvir Arafat Khan   Senior Energy Storage System Engineer, Hanwha Q Cells America Limited, Palo Alto, USA

Abhishek Shukla   Dr A P J Abdul Kalam Technical University, India

Rezaul Azim   Professor, University of Chittagong, Bangladesh

Jinfeng Li   Imperial College London and University of Southampton, UK

Muhammad Aamir   Professor, Faculty of Engineering, Sir Syed University of Engineering and Technology, Pakistan

Muhammad Saddam Khokhar   Postdoctoral Research Fellow, School of Computer Science & Information Technology, Jiangsu University, China

Man Fung Lo   Lecturer, Department of Mathematics and Information Technology, The Education University of Hong Kong, Hong Kong SAR, China

Amando Jr. Pimentel   Higher College of Technology, Muscat, Oman

Contents

Cloud, IoT and Distributed Computing

An Evaluation of the Correlation Between Task Characteristics and Input Data Size in Scientific Workflows

Taichi Sugimura[✉] and Takahiro Koita

Graduate School of Science and Engineering, Doshisha University, 1-3 Tatara Miyakodani, Kyotanabe 610-0394, Kyoto, Japan
ctwg0138@mail4.doshisha.ac.jp, tkoita@mail.doshisha.ac.jp

Abstract. With the recent spread of commercial cloud environments, the execution of scientific workflows in cloud environments has been attracting attention. Because commercial cloud environment platforms provide over several hundred types of computing resources of varied performance, it is difficult to determine which computing resources are appropriate for execution. In this study, we evaluate the correlation between task characteristics and task input data size when Montage is executed on multiple instance types on Amazon EC2 (Elastic Compute Cloud) to predict task characteristics in advance from information that can be obtained before execution. Previous research has shown how to predict task characteristics from input data size. We use run time, input/output (I/O) read/write volume, and maximum memory consumption as task characteristics. We executed Montage on five different instances of EC2 using three data size patterns. As a result, we found a tendency in VolumeReadBytes by task and execution order and, with the exception of c5.xlarge, all task characteristics were highly correlated with VolumeReadBytes.

Keywords: Amazon EC2 · Scientific workflows · Task characteristics

1 Introduction

With the recent diffusion of commercial cloud environments, the execution of scientific workflows in cloud environments have been attracting attention [1, 2, 15, 16]. However, it is difficult to determine which computing resources are appropriate for executing scientific workflows because commercial cloud providers provide over several hundred computing resources of varied performance [3].

Scientific workflows consist of multiple tasks, each of which has different characteristics (task characteristics) in terms of run time, input/output (I/O) usage volume (I/O read/write volume), and memory consumption.

In this study, we use Amazon Elastic Compute Cloud (EC2) as the commercial cloud environment [4]. The computing resources of EC2 are called instances. EC2 provides multiple instance types and the combination of CPU, memory, storage, and network capacity differs for each instance type.

© ICST Institute for Computer Sciences, Social Informatics and Telecommunications Engineering 2023
Published by Springer Nature Switzerland AG 2023. All Rights Reserved
M. H. Miraz et al. (Eds.): iCETiC 2022, LNICST 463, pp. 3–13, 2023.
https://doi.org/10.1007/978-3-031-25161-0_1

The above shows that the EC2 where a given scientific workflow is varies in terms of the cost and time required for execution depending on the instance in which it is executed. Therefore, several algorithms have been proposed to predict in advance which instance is appropriate for the EC2 user's desired cost and time [5, 17]. These algorithms assume that accurate estimates of task characteristics are available, but such estimates are difficult to generate in practice [6, 12–14].

Therefore, the purpose of this study is to show the correlation between the input data size that can be obtained before task execution and the task characteristics when the task is executed, based on the study by Silva et al.

Table 1. Basis for correlation between I/O reads and estimated target task characteristics.

Task characteristics correlated with I/O read volume	Basis
Run time	If a task performs a series of calculations on each value of the input data, it is correlated with the input data size
I/O write volume	If the task is applying a transformation to the input data, it is correlated with the input data size, which is constant if the output data is a summary of the input data
Maximum memory consumption	Input data is usually read into a data structure in memory for processing and thus correlates with the input data size

Table 2. Mean and standard deviation of actual measured values of task characteristics when input data size is varied in three patterns (Some data are shown with modifications).

Task	Run time		I/O read volume		I/O write volume		Maximum memory consumption	
	Mean (s)	Std. Dev.	Mean (MB)	Std. Dev.	Mean (MB)	Std. Dev.	Mean (MB)	Std. Dev.
mProjectPP	1.40	0.51	0.67	0.96	5.29	7.60	7.67	11.01
mDiffFit	0.14	0.99	4.39	7.31	0.36	0.85	12.22	19.03
mConcatFit	40.80	51.33	1.76	4.04	2.33	1.94	18.99	0.82
mBgModel	677.71	535.44	0.96	0.76	0.33	1.60	32.70	9.02

(continued)

Table 2. (*continued*)

Task	Run time		I/O read volume		I/O write volume		Maximum memory consumption	
	Mean (s)	Std. Dev.	Mean (MB)	Std. Dev.	Mean (MB)	Std. Dev.	Mean (MB)	Std. Dev.
mBackground	0.11	0.16	2.71	3.87	5.36	7.87	9.20	13.13
mImgtbl	0.50	1.13	1.85	1.10	0.96	14.97	20.17	1.42
mAdd	14.92	29.32	1207.50	515.15	1520.62	467.76	34.11	4.62
mShrink	3.05	2.01	430.02	65.65	2.07	2.55	16.92	1.51
mJPEG	0.46	0.21	24.15	2.29	0.49	0.19	15.67	1.33

Table 3. Pearson's correlation coefficient (ρ) of run time, I/O write volume, and maximum memory consumption for I/O read volume.

Task	ρ		
	run time	I/O write volume	maximum memory consumption
mProjectPP	-0.01	0.99	0.99
mDiffFit	-0.01	0.80	0.96
mConcatFit	0.64	0.36	0.12
mBgModel	0.95	-0.02	0.97
mBackground	0.03	0.97	0.99
mImgtbl	0.55	0.00	0.13
mAdd	0.57	0.82	0.81
mShrink	0.55	0.04	-0.12
mJPEG	0.05	-0.15	0.99

2 Previous Study

Silva et al. proposed a method for predicting task characteristics from input data size. Their study examines the correlation between I/O read volume and estimated target task characteristics (run time, I/O write volume, and memory consumption) based on the assumption that input data size and I/O read volume are approximately equal. Their study is based on the assumptions shown in Table 1.

Table 2 shows Silva et al.'s experimental results, specifically the mean and standard deviation of the run time, I/O read/write volume, and maximum memory consumption for each task when the Montage input data size is varied in three different patterns [7].

Table 3 shows the Pearson's correlation coefficients (ρ) of run time, I/O write volume, and maximum memory consumption for I/O read volume obtained from the measurements in the Silva et al. experiment. Cells showing a high correlation coefficient with an absolute value of 0.80 or higher for I/O read volume are gray colored. The threshold value of 0.80 was chosen somewhat arbitrarily from Silva et al.'s measured values.

In our study, the experiment follows the following 1–3 steps of Silva et al.'s study and adds a fourth.

1. Input data size can be varied in 3 patterns.
2. Measure run time, I/O read/write volume, and maximum memory consumption.
3. Calculate Pearson's correlation coefficients of run time, I/O write volume, and maximum memory consumption for I/O read volume from experimental measurements.
4. Measure task characteristics across multiple instance types.

Table 4. Montage task structure.

Task	Processed contents
mHdr	Create FITS header template from parameters
mArchiveDownload	Download RAW images in FITS format from astronomy missions
mImgtbl(raw)	Extract FITS header information from a set of files and create an ASCII image metadata table
mProjExec	Reproject each image in the image metadata table to the scale defined in the FITS header template file
mImgtbl(projected)	Extract FITS header information from a set of files and create an ASCII image metadata table
mAdd	Run and load the reprojected image with the same mImgtbl list used for reprojection, using the same FITS header template
mViewer	Create PNG or JPEG images from one or more FITS images

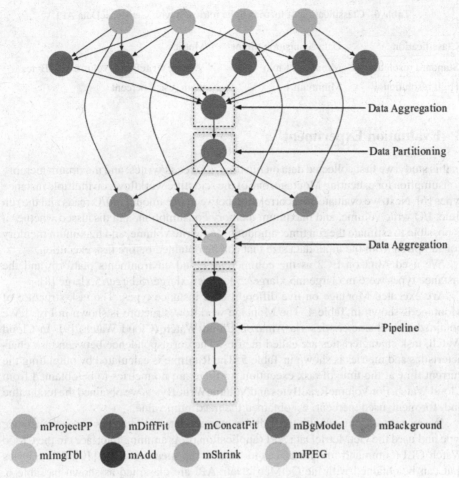

Fig. 1. The Montage workflow structure [11].

Table 5. Correspondence between task characteristics and metrics.

Task Characteristics	Metrics	Unit
Run time	N/A	Second (s)
I/O read volume	VolumeReadBytes	Megabyte (MB)
I/O write volume	VolumeWriteBytes	Megabyte (MB)
Maximum memory consumption	mem_used_percent	Percent (%)

Table 6. Classification of metrics to be retrieved with GetMetricData API.

Classification	Data acquisition timing	Metrics
Standard resolution	Minimum 1 min	VolumeWriteBytes/VolumeReadBytes
High resolution	Minimum 1 s	mem_used_percent

3   Evaluation Experiment

In this study, we first collected data on run time, I/O reads/writes, and maximum memory consumption for executing Montage, one of the scientific workflows on multiple instance types [6]. Next, we evaluated the correlation between the amount of I/O reads and the run time, I/O write volume, and maximum memory consumption, and discussed whether it is possible to estimate the run time, amount of I/O write volume, and maximum memory consumption from the input data size that can be obtained before task execution.

We used Amazon EC2 as the commercial cloud environments platform and the instance types were m5.large/m5.xlarge/c5.large/c5.xlarge/r5.large/r5.xlarge [8].

We executed Montage on five different EC2 instance types. The task structure of Montage is shown in Table 4. The Montage workflow structure is shown in Fig. 1.We obtained task characteristics via Amazon Cloud Watch (Cloud Watch) [9]. In Cloud Watch, task characteristics are called metrics. The correspondence between task characteristics and metrics is shown in Table 5. The Runtime is calculated by outputting the current time at the time of task execution, so there are no metrics to be obtained from Cloud Watch. For VolumeReadBytes and VolumeWriteBytes, we obtained the total value and, for mem_used_percent, we obtained the maximum value.

We executed Montage with three different input data size patterns for each instance type and used the GetMetricData API (application programming interface) in the Cloud Watch CLI (command line interface) to acquire the measurements [10]. The metrics that can be obtained with the GetMetricData API are classified as shown in Table 6. For standard resolution metrics, the minimum timing for obtaining measurements is one minute. Some of the tasks in our experiments have a Runtime of less than one minute, so, when the standard resolution metrics for these tasks are retrieved with GetMetricData API, the metrics for the other tasks are added together. Therefore, in this study, we added a process to "stop task execution for one minute" between each task.

Table 7. Mean and standard deviation of actual measured values of task characteristics when input data size is varied in three patterns.

Task	Runtime		VolumeReadBytes		VolumeWriteBytes		mem_used_percent	
	Mean (s)	Std. Dev.	Mean (MB)	Std. Dev.	Mean (MB)	Std. Dev.	Mean (%)	Std. Dev.
(a) m5.large								
Preliminary arrangements	0.00	0.00	1.00	1.00	65.49	65.24	2.38	0.38
mHdr	2.50	0.50	0.00	0.00	0.32	0.11	2.76	0.00
mArchiveDownload	416.50	341.50	0.00	0.00	379.70	324.37	2.79	0.01
mImgtbl(raw)	6.50	4.50	0.03	0.03	16.65	8.25	2.80	0.01
mProjExec	187.00	159.00	0.01	0.01	1783.85	1514.44	18.94	12.25
mImgtbl (projected)	0.50	0.50	0.00	0.00	12.78	12.50	18.95	12.25
mAdd	7.50	6.50	91.62	91.62	1037.17	829.48	19.00	12.27
mViewer	43.00	35.00	2.42	1.75	27.67	20.60	32.06	30.05
(b) m5.xlarge								
Preliminary arrangements	0.00	0.00	1.03	1.45	76.93	108.35	1.32	0.15
mHdr	2.67	0.47	16.08	22.74	3.36	3.77	1.47	0.01
mArchiveDownload	648.00	90.05	0.00	0.00	689.42	21.63	1.48	0.00
mImgtbl(raw)	10.67	0.47	0.03	0.04	22.57	21.42	1.49	0.00
mProjExec	344.00	0.00	0.00	0.00	3170.66	134.89	15.48	0.00
mImgtbl (projected)	1.33	0.47	0.00	0.00	152.79	134.52	15.48	0.00
mAdd	12.67	0.47	0.00	0.00	1123.20	807.71	15.57	0.00
mViewer	79.00	0.00	0.22	0.31	775.94	815.73	30.36	0.49
(c) c5.xlarge								
Preliminary arrangements	0.00	0.00	16.84	2.85	37.94	52.73	2.20	0.28
mHdr	2.33	0.47	4.37	4.75	62.23	87.49	2.62	0.11
mArchiveDownload	654.33	35.56	17.75	21.56	705.93	16.43	2.72	0.19
mImgtbl(raw)	10.00	0.00	0.03	0.04	9.91	13.11	2.74	0.19
mProjExec	214.00	140.71	0.02	0.02	3237.16	78.50	31.65	0.21
mImgtbl (projected)	1.33	0.47	0.00	0.00	86.045	78.28	31.66	0.21
mAdd	12.33	0.47	159.54	63.80	1695.98	241.16	31.79	0.22
mViewer	71.33	0.47	4.47	0.45	203.10	253.27	59.30	5.42
(d) r5.xlarge								
Preliminary arrangements	0.00	0.00	0.70	0.99	77.16	77.21	0.68	0.08
mHdr	2.33	0.47	0.00	0.00	1.21	0.69	0.75	0.02
mArchiveDownload	654.67	100.13	16.08	22.74	672.30	20.60	0.76	0.01

(*continued*)

Table 7. (*continued*)

Task	Runtime		VolumeReadBytes		VolumeWriteBytes		mem_used_percent	
	Mean (s)	Std. Dev.	Mean (MB)	Std. Dev.	Mean (MB)	Std. Dev.	Mean (%)	Std. Dev.
mImgtbl(raw)	10.33	0.47	0.03	0.04	42.10	16.81	0.77	0.00
mProjExec	345.00	1.41	0.00	0.00	2952.02	152.84	7.24	0.20
mImgtbl (projected)	2.00	0.00	0.00	0.00	371.40	152.85	7.72	0.00
mAdd	12.00	0.00	0.00	0.00	333.52	470.86	7.72	0.00
mViewer	79.67	0.00	0.22	0.99	1549.76	77.21	14.82	0.08

Table 8. Pearson's correlation coefficients (ρ) for each instance type of Montage execution. Cells with high correlation coefficients to VolumeReadBytes are gray colored. N/A is when VolumeReadBytes or Runtime/mem_used_percent/VolumeWriteBytes have the same value.

(a) m5.large

Task	ρ		
	Runtime	Volume-WriteBytes	mem_used_percent
preliminary arrangements	N/A	1.00	1.00
mHdr	N/A	N/A	N/A
mArchiveDownload	N/A	N/A	N/A
mImgtbl(raw)	-1.00	1.00	-1.00
mProjExec	-1.00	-1.00	-1.00
mImgtbl(projected)	N/A	N/A	N/A
mAdd	1.00	1.00	1.00
mViewer	1.00	1.00	1.00

(b) m5.xlarge

Task	ρ		
	Runtime	Volume-WriteBytes	mem_used_percent
preliminary arrangements	N/A	1.00	0.24
mHdr	-1.00	1.00	-0.92
mArchiveDownload	N/A	N/A	N/A
mImgtbl(raw)	0.50	0.96	-0.85
mProjExec	N/A	N/A	N/A
mImgtbl(projected)	N/A	N/A	N/A
mAdd	N/A	N/A	N/A
mViewer	N/A	0.99	0.41

(*continued*)

Table 8. (*continued*)

(c) c5.xlarge

Task	ρ		
	Runtime	Volume-WriteBytes	mem_used_percent
preliminary arrangements	N/A	-0.53	0.69
mHdr	-0.34	-0.34	0.20
mArchiveDownload	-0.85	0.69	0.94
mImgtbl(raw)	N/A	-0.50	0.95
mProjExec	0.76	0.94	-0.49
mImgtbl(projected)	N/A	N/A	N/A
mAdd	0.99	-0.99	1.00
mViewer	-0.52	1.00	0.53

(d) r5.xlarge

Task	ρ		
	Runtime	Volume-WriteBytes	mem_used_percent
preliminary arrangements	N/A	0.97	0.08
mHdr	N/A	N/A	N/A
mArchiveDownload	-0.94	0.99	-1.00
mImgtbl(raw)	-0.50	-0.98	0.91
mProjExec	N/A	N/A	N/A
mImgtbl(projected)	N/A	N/A	N/A
mAdd	N/A	N/A	N/A
mViewer	-0.50	-1.00	0.86

4   Results and Discussion

Table 7 shows the mean and standard deviation of Runtime, VolumeReadBytes, VolumeWriteBytes, and mem_used_percent for each task for each instance type when the input data size is varied in three patterns. The values for c5.large were not measured because the disk ran out of space during task execution for all input data sizes measured. Table 7 shows that VolumeReadBytes is 0 for mImgtbl(projected) for all four instance types in which it is presumed that the FITS (flexible image transit system) header information extracted by mImgtbl(raw) was cached in memory and reused. VolumeReadBytes became 0 for the two instance types on mHdr, mArchiveDownload, mProjExec, and mAdd. We will examine these factors in the future, taking into consideration the characteristics between instance types and instance families. In m5.xlarge/r5.large/r5.xlarge, VolumeReadBytes became 0 for all tasks after the second execution of Montage on the same instance, indicating that the memory cache is effective on these instance types. The following table shows the results of the analysis.

Table 8 shows the Pearson's correlation coefficients between VolumeReadBytes and task characteristics for each instance type. The absolute value of the correlation coefficient for m5.large is 1 because of insufficient disk space in one of the three input data size patterns.

5 Conclusions

In this study, we investigated the correlation between the input data size that can be obtained before task execution and the task characteristics when the task is actually executed, based on the background that it is difficult to generate estimates of task characteristics. In the experiment, we obtained data on run time, I/O read/write volume, and maximum memory consumption when Montage, a scientific workflow, was executed with multiple instance types. As a result, we discovered a tendency in VolumeReadBytes by task and execution order and, with the exception of c5.xlarge, all task characteristics had a high correlation with VolumeReadBytes. In the future, we will increase the number of input data size patterns to be varied and investigate the factors causing the correlation.

References

1. Hoffa, C., et al.: On the use of cloud computing for scientific workflows. In: Proceedings of the Fourth IEEE International Conference on eScience, pp. 640–645 (2008)
2. Scientific Workflows. https://link.springer.com/referenceworkentry/10.1007/978-0-387-39940-9_1471. Accessed 17 July 2022
3. Juve, G., Deelman, E., Berriman, G.B., Berman, B.P., Maechling, P.: An evaluation of the cost and performance of scientific workflows on amazon EC2. J. Grid Comput. **10**, 5–21 (2012)
4. Amazon.com: Elastic Compute Cloud. http://aws.amazon.com/ec2. Accessed 17 July 2022
5. Ibrahim, E., El-Bahnasawy, N.A., Omara, F.A.: Task scheduling algorithm in cloud computing environment based on cloud pricing models. In: Proceedings of the World Symposium on Computer Applications & Research, pp. 65–71 (2016)
6. da Silva, R.F., Juve, G., Rynge, M., Deelman, E., Livny, M.: Online task resource consumption prediction for scientific workflows. Parallel Process. Lett. **25**(3), 1541003 (2015)
7. Montage. http://montage.ipac.caltech.edu/. Accessed 17 July 2022
8. Shiraishi, R.: A consideration on computational resource selection using task characteristics. Graduation thesis of Doshisha University (2018)
9. AWS Cloud Watch. https://aws.amazon.com/jp/cloudwatch/. Accessed 17 July 2022
10. AWS Cloud Watch, GetMetricData API. https://docs.aws.amazon.com/ja_jp/AmazonCloudWatch/latest/APIReference/API_GetMetricData.html. Accessed 17 July 2022
11. Bharathi, S., Chervenak, A., Deelman, E., Mehta, G., Su, M., Vahi, K.: Characterization of scientific workflows. In: Proceedings of the Third Workshop on Workflows in Support of Large-Scale Science, pp. 1–10 (2008)
12. Pham, T., Durillo, J.J., Fahringer, T.: Predicting workflow task execution time in the cloud using a two-stage machine learning approach. IEEE Trans. Cloud Comput. **8**(1), 256–268 (2020)
13. Hilman, M.H., Rodriguez, M.A., Buyya, R.: Task runtime prediction in scientific workflows using an online incremental learning approach. In: Proceedings of the IEEE/ACM 11th International Conference on Utility and Cloud Computing, pp. 93–102 (2018)
14. Arunarani, A.R., Manjula, D., Sugumaran, V.: Task scheduling techniques in cloud computing: a literature survey. Futur. Gener. Comput. Syst. **91**, 407–415 (2019)
15. Ostermann, S., Iosup, A., Yigitbasi, N., Prodan, R., Fahringer, T., Epema, D.: A performance analysis of EC2 cloud computing services for scientific computing. In: Avresky, D.R., Diaz, M., Bode, A., Ciciani, B., Dekel, E. (eds.) Cloud Computing, vol. 34, pp. 115–131. Springer, Heidelberg (2009). https://doi.org/10.1007/978-3-642-12636-9_9

16. Liew, C.S., Atkinson, M.P., Galea, M., Ang, T.F., Martin, P., Hemert, J.V.: Scientific workflows, moving across paradigms. ACM Comput. Surv. **49**, 1–39 (2017)
17. Su, S., Li, J., Huang, Q., Huang, X., Shuang, K., Wang, J.: Cost-efficient task scheduling for executing large programs in the cloud. Parallel Comput. **39**, 177–188 (2013)

Evaluation of Semantic Interoperability of Automotive Service API Models Based on Metamodels Similarity Metrics Using a Semi-automated Approach

Sangita De[1,3]([⊠]) [iD], Juergen Mottok[2], and Přemek Brada[3]

[1] Volkswagen AG, Ingolstadt, Germany
sangita.de@outlook.de
[2] OstBayerische Technical Hochschule (OTH), Regensburg, Germany
[3] University of West Bohemia, Pilsen, Czech Republic

Abstract. In recent years, mapping of application software components' ontologies semantically emerged as a big research challenge in automotive application domain that manipulates several cross-enterprise synergy knowledge application frameworks. The same knowledge formalized by different experts in different vehicle application frameworks leads to heterogeneous representations of components' interface data. Consequently, this causes the most daunting impediment in semantic interoperability between the service components in cooperative automotive systems. From a modeling perspective, in the absence of standardized domain-based unified modeling techniques, the orchestration and resolution of semantic data interoperability between various vehicle application frameworks' components' interface models remain a challenge. However, this challenge could be addressed using ontological metamodeling by specifying semantic associations between components' interface model concepts based on the domain knowledge. Apart from the semantic mapping of interface ontological metamodels, this work also defines quality metrics to determine the degree of semantic alignment achieved between the various interface ontologies. Additionally, to reduce development time and cost towards semantic interoperability, this work proposes a semi-automated plugin tool for the applicability of the evaluated quality metrics to semantic mapping of real-world components' interface models.

Keywords: Framework · Interface · Metamodel · Metrics · Ontology · Semantic

1 Introduction

1.1 Motivation

In the past decade, semantics have greatly benefited the research of services integration, search, data linking, and analysis of data in the semantic web domain. In the vehicle domain, multiple cross-enterprise frameworks' service interfaces and their specific

M. H. Miraz et al. (Eds.): iCETiC 2022, LNICST 463, pp. 14–28, 2023.
https://doi.org/10.1007/978-3-031-25161-0_2

vocabularies of terms causes impediments to semantic interoperability between various service components. Semantic mapping exploration based on domain knowledge can be a key solution in allowing efficient resolution of data heterogeneity [2].

Ontologies explicitly represent domains that are composed of various entities, properties, and relationships that exist in the real world. In fact, ontologies can be used to specify heterogeneously structured framework-specific databases with comparable semantics in a formal way [6].

To simplify mapping of heterogeneous vehicle service Software Component (SWCs) interface data semantically, hence, it is substantial to emphasize mainly on the generic interface semantic traits and avoid those platform-specific details that are not mandatory for the interoperability of the interfaces [14]. Therefore, from a domain modeling perspective based on OMG standards [1], this research work proposes the abstraction of the real-world automotive systems SWCs' interfaces models that represent the M1 Modeling Layer to ontological metamodels that represent the M2 Modeling Layer to be more formalized with a focus on semantic traits of Component-Port-Connector (CPC) features.

The quality of semantic alignment achieved by mapping between the interface ontological metamodel determines the degree of compatibility among the heterogeneous application frameworks service SWCs' models in automotive domain for services collaboration. To evaluate the quality of semantic alignment in terms of cohesion and coupling between the interface ontological metamodels [3] concepts and instances, there are few metrics proposed and evaluated manually using few running examples in the current scope of this paper. The ontologies in the current scope are described using OWL (Ontology Web Language).

To tackle the semantic interoperability issue from an evolutionary perspective in an ever-growing vehicle domain, the focus of this research paper is to also utilize the already obtained quantitative values of semantic alignment quality metrics that are evaluated between framework API (Application Program Interface) ontological metamodels (M2 Modeling Layer) to determine the semantic mappings between the real-world software systems SWCs' interface models (M1 Modeling Layer) using a semi-automated design approach. The proposed design approach also reduces human intervention and decreases in time and effort that will otherwise be required by vehicle service users to semantically map, align, and integrate new additional real-world SWC models to automotive cooperative software systems.

1.2 State of the Art

Based on a literature survey [1, 2], it emerges that semantic mapping between ontological metamodel entities to resolve heterogeneity between different knowledge bases is a precondition to enhance the interoperability between services in automotive cooperative systems. Semantic mapping can be automatic, semi-automatic, or manual. From a domain modeling perspective, two common approaches can be used to achieve semantic interoperability using mapping. One approach includes merging one or multiple local framework ontologies to create a single global domain ontology with which all the semantic data are associated. Another approach includes mappings to establish semantic alignment among the source local ontologies using a mediator or reference ontology

[2]. The latter approach preserves the local knowledge base and is covered as part of the current research scope.

In the field of artificial intelligence, the GLUE project [8] is a research work that proposes an automatic mapping creation system that uses instances to determine which ontological concepts should be matched. However, since the proposed method works only on the instances limits its applicability to multiple cases. QOM (Quick Ontology Mapping) [4] is also a semi-automated system that is based on a mapper, namely, NOM (Naive Ontology Mapper) that aims at discovering mappings in a rapid way using a so-called hybrid mapping system, rather than maximizing the accuracy of those mappings. For ontology mapping in service-oriented systems, MAFRA [10] toolkit proposes and defines a notion of automatic semantic bridges for the specification of complex semantic mappings.

Both ontology and metamodel lay the foundational theory of ontological metamodeling, enabling the semantic expressiveness of metamodels and hence promoting semantic alignments and composability [1]. Ontological frameworks provide inferred reasoning between metamodel entities that further helps in identifying semantic correlations between them. However, in ontological metamodels, the metamodel and ontology are strongly coupled to each other, and hence, incurring a little evolution of the ontology may change the overall ontological metamodel structure.

Ontologies are expected to become progressively better in the future in the direction of reusability. Therefore, a systematic discipline of evaluation of ontology must be created to ensure the quality of the content [5, 6]. Overall, ontology quality metrics can be basically classified into three categories such as structural metrics, functional metrics, and usability profiling metrics. Burton-Jones et al. [4] proposed an approach to ontology evaluation from a quality-oriented perspective considering the usability profiling of the ontologies. This approach fundamentally describes ontology quality evaluation from a software engineering view, where internal attributes influence external quality attributes.

In automotive domain, ontologies are generally evaluated so far using structural metrics. To improvise the management of knowledge in an intelligent way inside the vehicle with multiple advanced complex functions and to also share the knowledge with other cars, authors et al. [7], describes a reference ontological model design with implicit reasoning to share and collaborate the knowledge between different in-vehicle functions and other vehicles using a common platform. This work does not include evaluation of the quality of semantic mapping between the collaborating vehicle services.

2   Design Methodology

2.1   Ontology Metrics for Semantic Alignment Quality Evaluation

This research work proposes two fundamental types of semantic mapping quality evaluation metrics based on cohesion and coupling [3] between vehicle SWCs' interface ontological metamodels. The first category is the schema metrics that address the semantic alignment between concepts interface ontology schemas, and the second category is the knowledgebase metrics that evaluates the semantic alignment between individuals of ontology classes existing within the knowledge base [9, 13].

The Semantic Similarity Schema Metric: For an automotive SWC API ontology schema, for example OB, the Semantic Similarity Schema (SSS) metric is represented as the percentage of the fraction of the number of semantically *equivalent* schema classes (EQVC) that is equivalent to the classes of interface ontology schemas of other SWC APIs semantically compared to the total number (TRC) of the schema classes in OB. From an ontology schema coverage view, TRC may include inheritance classes (IHCL), noninheritance classes (INHCL), as well as EQVC in the given schema OB [9].

$$SSS = EQVC/TRC \qquad (1)$$

And $TRC = IHCL + INHCL + EQVC$ in(1).

The Instance Relationship Richness Metric: The Instance Relationship Richness (IRR) metric represents the depth of knowledgebase. For an automotive SWC API ontology schema, for example, OB, IRR is represented as the percentage of the fraction of the number of *sameAs* instances (ISAI) of schema classes of OB compared to the total number of individuals of the given schema classes (TR_{Inst}) existing in OB. From an ontology schema instance coverage view, TR_{Inst} may include *sameAs* and *differentFrom* individuals (IDFI) of the schema classes [9, 13].

$$IRR = ISAI/TR_{Inst} \qquad (2)$$

And $TR_{Inst} = ISAI + IDFI$ in (2).

The Class Instance Connectivity Metric: For an automotive SWC API ontology schema, for example, OB, the Class Instance Connectivity (CIC) metric is represented as the percentage of the fraction of the number of *sameAs* individuals of semantically equivalent schema classes (EQSC) existing in OB compared to the total number of semantically equivalent schema classes (TRQC) existing in OB [9]. The value evaluated for this metric determine the degree of connectivity between the schema classes. This metric also fundamentally indicates the fraction of schema classes equivalence relationships that are being used at the individual level of the schema, for example, OBi to create *sameAs* relationships to ease interoperability at instance level [9, 13].

$$CIC = EQSC/TRQC \qquad (3)$$

And $EQSC \propto (sameAsINDIVIDUAL\ (OBI))$ in (3).

2.2 An Automotive Case Study

The automotive domain *case study* that is considered in the current research work is *Autonomous Maneuvering* from the ADAS (Advance Driver Assistance System) automotive functional domain. To realize such a *case study*, fundamental services collaborations between various automotive application framework components from cross-knowledge domains like automotive, robotics, infotainment, etc. are needed to accomplish the services requirements, as seen in Fig. 1. The commonly used automotive application frameworks service SWCs to realize such a *case study* are namely, AUTOSAR

Adaptive, Franca (from Genivi) and ROS2 (Robotics Operating system version 2) [9]. The service SWCs' interface metamodels of these three frameworks are accordingly named as **Source 1**, **Source 2**, and **Source 3** for semantic mapping. To establish interoperability and services collaboration among the given sources, it is substantial to identify semantic synergies among their application component frameworks' service API metamodels using a common domain-specific reference or *mediator* API metamodel [2]. Tracing of semantic synergies between API metamodels is done manually in the current research scope [9].

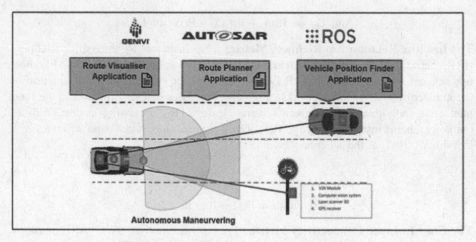

Fig. 1. Case study on autonomous maneuvering.

2.3   Overview of Semantic Mapping Strategy

Each local interface ontology represents a vehicle service component framework's interface metamodel's semantic data and is defined as a 4-tuple $IO = <C, S, I, A>$, where C is a finite set of Interface concepts; S is a finite set of semantic relations; I is a set of instances (or individuals); A is a set of axioms. From a vehicle domain modeling perspective, simulation modelers always concentrate on how to introduce the domain concepts and relations into a metamodel to enhance its semantic expressiveness [2]. The semantic mapping between different local interface ontologies is done by merging the ontologies together with a domain-specific *mediator* interface ontology, say, **DM,** into a global interface ontology, as seen in the given Fig. 2 [11]. It can be observed that,

- **OGI** represents the platform-independent and vehicle domain-specific, global interface ontology schema for automotive SWC APIs.
- **OPI** represents the local framework-specific interface conceptual ontology schemas.
- **RO** represents a platform-agnostic, vehicle domain-specific *mediator ontology. Mediator* ontology contains generic, vehicle domain-specific service components APIs'

semantic data that are common to most vehicle application frameworks. The *mediator* ontology acts as a common semantic ground to bridge the gaps between framework-specific semantic traits of local interface ontologies.

- *MPR* represents mappings between *OPI* and *RO*. Ω is a set of mapping axioms between *RO* and *OPI* which includes, for example, mapping of interface semantic concepts.
- *MGS* defines mappings between global ontology *OGI* and local ontology *OPI*. ¥ is a set of mapping axioms between each *OPI* schema and global schema *OGI*.
- *QGI* represents queries that can be propagate in mainly two directions: (1) the data-integration direction, from the global ontology the queries are further broken into small subqueries and passed over the multiple local sources, and (2) the peer-to-peer direction, where the query on some local interface ontology source schema is propagated further to other local interface ontology schema sources through the commonly connected global ontology.

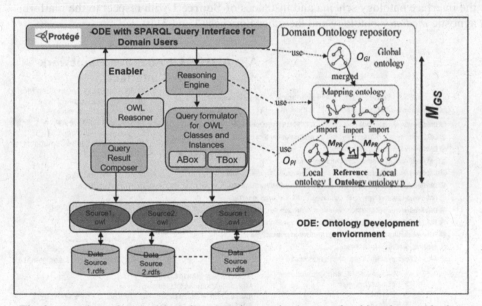

Fig. 2. Workflow of methodology for semantic mapping between local interface ontologies.

Each of the local interface ontology sources must follow a defined set of SWRL (Semantic Web Rule Language) inference mapping rules to map its semantic data with other local interface ontology sources. A few examples of the SWRL inference rules that are commonly used for the semantic mapping of interface ontology sources can be seen in the below equations. In Eq. (4), **R** represents a relational property by which object **x** is related to object **y** and to object **z**, which implies that **y** is *sameAs* **z**. In Eq. (5), Class **A** and Class **B** are *subclasses* of Class **C**, and **m** is a common member element of Class **A** and **B**, which implies that **m** is also a member of Class **C** [9].

$$\mathbf{R(x, y)} \wedge \mathbf{R(x, z)} \rightarrow \mathbf{y = z} \tag{4}$$

$$A(m) \wedge B(m) \rightarrow C(m) \tag{5}$$

The automated generated implicit reasoning for interface ontology semantic mapping is further extended using query language like SPARQL for the verification of the semantic alignments between the local ontologies sources in the considered *case study*.

2.4 Evaluation Metrics for Interface Ontological Metamodels

The three-framework-specific SWCs' interface model sources associated with the given *case study* in Subsect. 2.2 are modeled as **Source1, Source 2,** and **Source 3** ontological metamodels based on CPC artifacts. The *inferred* semantic *equivalence* class axioms (*TBox axioms*) and *sameAs* instance axioms (*ABox axioms)* which are automatically generated by the reasoner of the ontology framework based on SWRL inference rules, are then identified. Figure 3 illustrates the inferred *TBox axioms* and *ABox axioms* between the interface ontology schema and instances of **Source 1** with respect to the platform-agnostic *mediator* ontology and the other **Sources** (**2** and **3**) [9, 12].

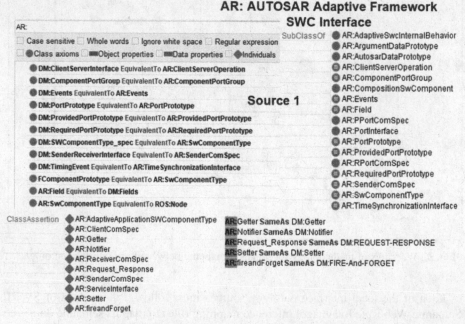

Fig. 3. Overview of inferred semantic axioms of interface ontology Source 1.

Like **Source 1**, the generated inferred semantic axioms are also identified for **Source 2** and **Source 3** both at ontology schema and individual levels, as seen in Fig. 4 and Fig. 5. The generated inferred semantic axioms can be utilized to empirically evaluate the semantic alignment quality metrics **SSS**, **IRR** and **CIC** for each interface ontology sources based on the cohesion and coupling between the sources [3]. The degree of semantic alignment between the given interfaces ontology sources of the *case study* is evaluated manually by the percentage of the semantic alignment quality metrics on a scale of 100 [9].

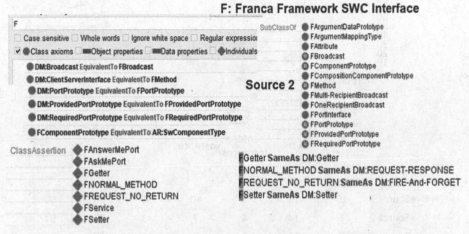

Fig. 4. Overview of inferred semantic axioms of interface ontology Source 2.

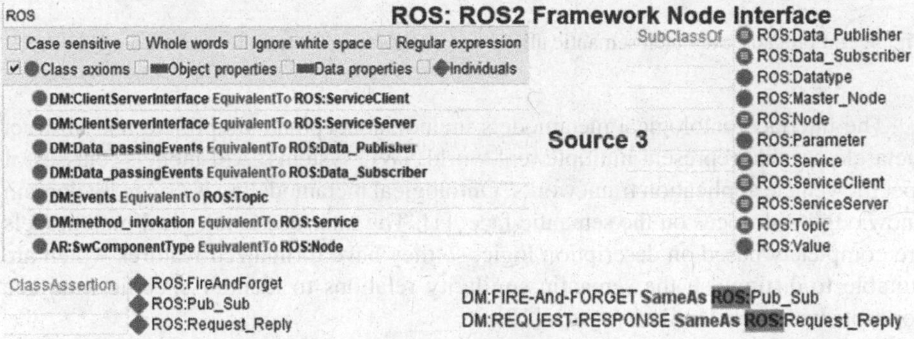

Fig. 5. Overview of inferred semantic axioms of interface ontology Source 3.

Based on the manual analysis, as seen in Fig. 6, for the interface ontological meta-model sources of the considered *case study*, **Source 1**, **Source 2**, and **Source 3**, it is observed that **Source 3** has the maximum values for **SSS**, and **IRR** metrics as evaluated. However, for **Source 2**, due to a smaller number of instances of schema classes, the knowledgebase data represents only limited knowledge of the source schema. Based on the evaluation criteria for each semantic alignment quality metric, the mean value is considered the *threshold* for that metric. The *threshold* for **SSS** = 52.3, **IRR** = 58, and **CIC** = 48.6. In Fig. 6, the values of the quality metrics (in percentages) which are above the *threshold* imply higher degrees of semantic alignment quality of the sources [3].

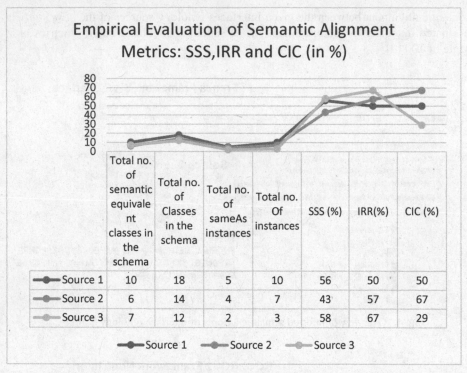

Fig. 6. Empirically evaluated semantic alignment quality metrics for interface ontology sources.

The interface ontological metamodels include conceptual, simplified, and abstract meta-classes that represent multiple real-world SWC systems' API models' classes of specific vehicle application frameworks. Ontological metamodeling is driven by domain knowledge with focus on the semantic facet [1]. The interface ontological metamodels are completely based on description logic, so they have formalized features which are suitable to distinguish the semantic similarity relations to identify specific interface concepts within the similarity space [12].

However, as seen in the past decades, the increase in demand for SoC (Service Oriented Communication) in the vehicle domain results in an increase in demand for the frequent addition of multiple heterogeneous vehicle service component models of third-party application frameworks into automotive cooperative systems to realize complex vehicle functionalities. Therefore, with this given evolution scenario, it is truly substantial from a time and effort optimization perspective to utilize or apply the achieved evaluated values of the semantic alignment quality metrics for the abstract, conceptual SWCs' interface metamodels (*M2 Modeling Layer*) at real-world system SWCs API models (*M1 Modeling Layer*) interaction level. This would reduce the reworks of service users in semantic alignment and integration of new additional real-world SWCs' API models into automotive cooperative systems, as illustrated in Fig. 7 [3].

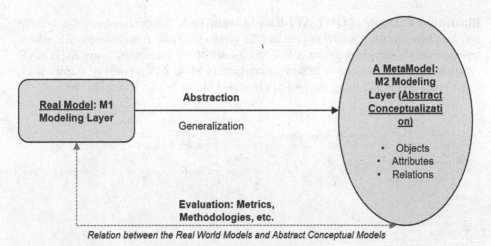

Relation between the Real World Models and Abstract Conceptual Models

Fig. 7. Evaluation of ontological metamodels as abstract representation of real-world models.

2.5 Applicability of Evaluated Semantic Alignment Quality Metrics to Real-World SWC Interface Models Using Semi-automated Approach

With the immense growth in the demand for the third-party services in the automotive domain, let us consider a scenario where a service consumer SWC of framework A wants to interact with a service provider SWC of framework B. Despite semantic commonalities in their interface methods, the difference in the frameworks' API specifications causes impediments in the interaction of the API models. Moreover, an emerging discomfort in the direction of service compatibility for services collaboration is that the service consumer framework experts usually fail to understand the service provider SWC's API model on the other end of the communication link and cannot invest required time to identify the possible semantic synergies between API models of SWCs of framework A and B by semantic mapping [12].

For the considered scenario to ease the interoperability between the real-world SWCs' API models of framework A and B by semantic mapping and proper orchestration, this research work proposes an automated OWL API-based *vehicle service choreography* tool that can be used as a plugin in Protégé. The tool has an eclipse-based user interface that allows users like the service consumers and service providers to specify their real-world SWC's API models from different application frameworks to be expressed as standardized ontologies, and then the tool automatically aligns the user-specified SWC's API models' semantic data based on the already achieved values of semantic alignment quality metrics for the abstract, conceptual interface ontological metamodels [13]. That is, in this case, the tool first checks the already achieved values of metrics for semantic alignment quality between interface ontological metamodels of framework A and framework B, and then based on these values of the metrics, the tool automatically *asserts* semantic relational axioms like *equivalence*, *sameAs*, *SubClassOf*, etc. between the users' specified real-world SWCs' API ontological models [9].

Illustrative Example of OWL API-Based Plugin Tool. To demonstrate the *vehicle service choreography* tool, let us consider the given *case study* from Subsect. 2.2, where a real system's service provider SWC API model of the framework, say, AUTOSAR Adaptive wants to interact with service consumers SWC API models of frameworks, say, Franca and ROS2 using the tool as illustrated in Fig. 8, Fig. 9 and Fig. 10.

```
********* User Choice Components Entry Section ********
Enter the number of SWCs whose APIs to be specified in generic template in digits (1...9):
3
**** Service Sowftware Component API Specifications*****
Enter the Name of the Automotive Service Framework whose SWC API needs to specified in standardized Ontology
  1. Autosar_Adaptive
  2.Franca
  3.ROS
  4.Android
  5.Cloud9
Autosar_Adaptive
  Enter The name of the Service SWC Type:
AutoSpeedSensor
Enter the number for the respective Communication Paradigm:
  1. REST
  2. RPC
  3. Event-Based
2
Enter the number for the Service Interface Type:
  1. SenderReceiver
  2.ClientServer
2
Enter the name for the Service Interface RPC Method:
GetTachoData
Method Successfully created!
Enter the name Service Instances:
DataRead
```

Fig. 8. User-specified real-world SWC API model of framework AUTOSAR Adaptive.

```
Enter the Name of the Automotive Service Framework whose SWC API needs to specified in standardized Ontology
  1. Autosar_Adaptive
  2.Franca
  3.ROS
  4.Android
  5.Cloud9
Franca
  Enter The name of the Service SWC Type:
DisplayAutoSpeed
Enter the number for the respective Communication Paradigm:
  1. REST
  2. RPC
  3. Event-Based
2
Enter the number for the Service Interface Type:
  1. SenderReceiver
  2.ClientServer
2
Enter the name for the Service Interface RPC Method:
PrintAutoSpeedData
Method Successfully created!
Enter the name Service Instances:
AutoSpeedDataDisplayUnit
```

Fig. 9. User-specified real-world SWC API model of framework Franca.

Each user-specified service SWC API model is automatically translated to an equivalent structured ontology by the tool based on a standardized ontology template. The user must specify the service SWC API models based on six fundamental elements or features [12, 14].

```
Enter the Name of the Automotive Service Framework whose SWC API needs to specified in standardized Ontology
 1. Autosar_Adaptive
 2.Franca
 3.ROS
 4.Android
 5.Cloud9
ROS
 Enter The name of the Service SWC Type:
 FindVehiclePosition
 Enter the number for the respective Communication Paradigm:
 1. REST
 2. RPC
 3. Event-Based
 2
 Enter the number for the Service Interface Type:
 1. SenderReceiver
 2.ClientServer
 2
 Enter the name for the Service Interface RPC Method:
 ReadVehiclePosition
 Method Successfully created!
 Enter the name Service Instances:
 ReadPositionCoordinates
```

Fig. 10. User-specified real-world SWC API model of framework ROS2.

- *Service Interface Types*: Interfaces are provided by the service SWCs and constitute aggregation of operations. They can be of different types like *operation-based* and *data-passing* [12].
- *Instances Type*: They specify the instances of vehicle service interface models.
- *Interface Roles*: They specify service SWC API models as consumers or providers.
- *Interface Method Calls*: They specify method definitions including information on parameter types, etc. Common examples on *Interface Method Calls* are *ClientServer, Sender-Receiver*, event based *Publish-Subscribe, Fire-and-Forget, Broadcast,* etc.
- *Bindings*: They specify the protocol-driven communication paradigm that is used in different vehicle application frameworks to invoke the methods of an interface, for example, SOME/IP for RPC, HTTP for REST [14].
- *Service Ports*: the service SWCs can constitute a single or aggregation of ports. A port is an endpoint enabling access to an interface [14].

Based on the automated *asserted* axioms by the *vehicle service choreography* tool and the SWRL inference mapping rules, examples seen in Eq. (4) and Eq. (5), the reasoner of the ontology modeling framework generates automatically *inferred* axioms to align the user-specified SWCs' API models' concepts and instances further semantically, as observed in Fig. 11. The tool has a *mediator* which together with the reasoner of an ontology framework automatically semantically aligns the service SWCs' API models of different frameworks and from a users' perspective saves time and cost in mapping of heterogeneous API semantic models of SWCs for service interoperability [14]. To verify the achieved semantic alignments, the reasoning can be extended by executing SPARQL queries on the given user-specified SWC API models, as illustrated in Fig. 12, where *ClientServer* is a platform-agnostic *mediator* interface ontology class.

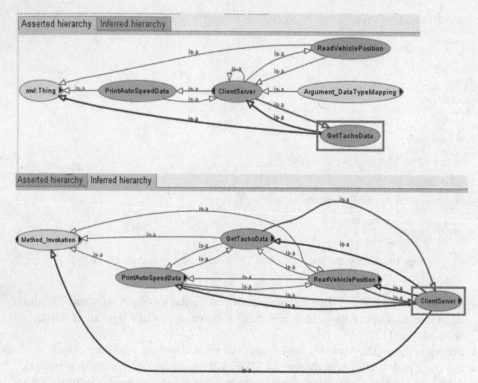

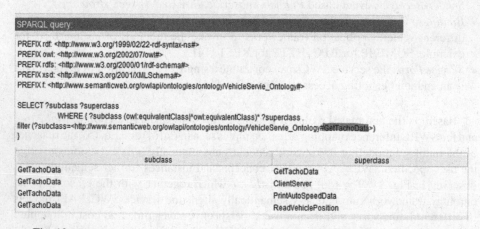

Fig. 11. Overview of semantic axioms identified between SWC API models using plugin Tool.

```
SPARQL query:

PREFIX rdf: <http://www.w3.org/1999/02/22-rdf-syntax-ns#>
PREFIX owl: <http://www.w3.org/2002/07/owl#>
PREFIX rdfs: <http://www.w3.org/2000/01/rdf-schema#>
PREFIX xsd: <http://www.w3.org/2001/XMLSchema#>
PREFIX f: <http://www.semanticweb.org/owlapi/ontologies/ontology/VehicleServie_Ontology#>

SELECT ?subclass ?superclass
        WHERE { ?subclass (owl:equivalentClass|^owl:equivalentClass)* ?superclass .
filter (?subclass=<http://www.semanticweb.org/owlapi/ontologies/ontology/VehicleServie_Ontology#GetTachoData>)
}
```

subclass	superclass
GetTachoData	GetTachoData
GetTachoData	ClientServer
GetTachoData	PrintAutoSpeedData
GetTachoData	ReadVehiclePosition

Fig. 12. Example of verification of semantic alignments of interface ontology sources.

3   Conclusion

Due to the lack of semantic interoperability between various vehicle services SWCs' interface data, recent years have seen in the automotive domain major impediment in

SoC (Service-oriented-Communication), especially in the direction of service discovery, service invocation, composing services and communications, etc. However, implementations of the measures to ease semantic interoperability were largely missing, not publicly available, or tailored to specific application needs. Ontology is an essential modeling technology that allows mapping data of heterogeneous frameworks' vehicle service SWCs' interfaces based on domain semantics. The semantic alignment between SWCs' API models using ontology not only ease interoperability between the API models but also paves the path for the reusability of the SWCs through their API models which is especially useful for automotive cooperative systems. The focus of this research work is on the exploration of semantic alignments between the local framework-specific ontologies within the vehicle domain using a mediator-centric approach. The apparent increase in demand for interoperability between various vehicle service SWCs' API models has led to an increase in the number of conceptual API ontological metamodels representations, which consequently has raised the necessity for evaluating the degree of semantic alignment quality between the API ontological metamodels sources to better understand the semantic interoperability and reusability of the sources. This is well evident from the proposed and evaluated semantic alignment quality metrics in this research work. Although the framework-specific API ontological metamodels are most preferred for semantic mapping and for evaluation of semantic alignment quality metrics, however, these metamodels are clumsy, generalized, and abstract from an evolution perspective. Therefore, this research work also focuses on using the evaluated values of the semantic alignment quality metrics of the interface ontological metamodels of various frameworks further for semantic mapping of real-world API models of the same frameworks to bridge the distance between the evaluation of abstract conceptualization and the real world using an automated OWL API based plugin tool. Additionally, from an evolution perspective, this would optimize time and effort in semantic alignment and integration of new SWC models in automotive cooperative systems. Nevertheless, more work is required in the directions of ontology and metrics coverage to evaluate interface semantic alignment quality in a broader scope in the future.

References

1. Yonglin, L., Zhi, Z., Qun, L.: An ontological metamodeling framework for semantic simulation model engineering. J. Syst. Eng. Electron. **31**(3), 527–538 (2020)
2. Poulain, T., Cullot, N., Yétongnon, K.: Ontology mapping specification in description logics for cooperative systems. J. des sciences pour l'ingénieur (JSPI) **7**, 64–71 (2006)
3. Hlomani, H., Stacey, D.: Approaches, methods, metrics, measures, and subjectivity in ontology evaluation: a survey. Semant. Web J. **1**(5), 1–11 (2014)
4. Ehrig, M., Staab, S.: QOM – quick ontology mapping. In: McIlraith, S.A., Plexousakis, D., van Harmelen, F. (eds.) ISWC 2004. LNCS, vol. 3298, pp. 683–697. Springer, Heidelberg (2004). https://doi.org/10.1007/978-3-540-30475-3_47
5. Burton-Jones, A., Storey, C.V., Sugumaran, V., Ahluwalia, P.: A semiotic metrics suite for assessing the quality of ontologies. Data Knowl. Eng. **55**(1), 84–102 (2005)
6. Obrst, L., Ceusters, W., Mani, I., Ray, S., Smith, B.: The Evaluation of Ontologies. In: Baker, C.J.O., Cheung, K.H. (eds.) Semantic Web, pp. 139–158. Springer, Boston (2007). https://doi.org/10.1007/978-0-387-48438-9_8

7. Feld, M., Müller, C.: The automotive ontology: managing knowledge inside the vehicle and sharing it between cars. In: Proceedings of 3rd International Conference on Automotive User Interfaces and Interactive Vehicular, pp. 79–86 (2011)
8. Doan, A., Madhavan, J., Domingos, P., Halevy, A.: Ontology matching: a machine learning approach. In: Staab, S., Studer, R. (eds.) Handbook on Ontologies. International Handbooks on Information Systems, pp. 385–403. Springer, Heidelberg (2004). https://doi.org/10.1007/978-3-540-24750-0_19
9. De, S., Brada, P., Mottok, J., Niklas, M.: The empirical evaluation of semantic alignment quality metrics for vehicle domain component frameworks interface ontologies. In: Proceedings of FLAIRS-34, Special Track: Semantic, Logics, Information Extraction and AI, vol. 34 (2021)
10. Silva, N., Rocha, J.: Service-oriented ontology mapping system. In: Proceedings of the Workshop on Semantic Integration of the International Semantic Web Conference, Sanibel Island (FL), USA (2003)
11. Hu, C., Zhang, X., Zhao, Q., Zhao, C.: Ontology-based semantic integration method for domain-specific scientific data. In: Eighth ACIS International Conference on Software Engineering, Artificial Intelligence, Networking, and Parallel/Distributed Computing (SNPD 2007), pp. 772–777 (2007)
12. Yahya, N., Md Taib, M.A.: An overview of service interface design approaches for interoperability of traditional system integration patterns. J. Comput. Res. Innov. 6(1), 44–53 (2021)
13. Tartir, S., Arpinar, I.B., Sheth, A.: Ontological evaluation and validation. In: Poli, R., Healy, M., Kameas, A. (eds.) Theory and Applications of Ontology: Computer Applications, pp. 115–130. Springer, Dordrecht (2010). https://doi.org/10.1007/978-90-481-8847-5_5
14. Bouhissi, H., Malki, M., Bouchiha. D.: Towards WSMO ontology specification from existing web services. In: CIIA. CEUR Workshop Proceedings, vol. 547. CEUR-WS.org (2009)

BCoT-Based Smart Manufacturing: An Enhanced Precise Measurement Management System

Mst. Surma Khatun[1], Aofan Liu[2(✉)], and Mahdi H. Miraz[2]

[1] ACCA global, Moscow, Russia
[2] Xiamen University Malaysia, Sepang, Selangor, Malaysia
SWE2009510@xmu.edu.my

Abstract. Blockchain with its transparent, decentralised and secured characteristics have surfaced it as a futuristic technology for a surplus of advanced industrial applications. Blockchain of Things (BCoT) is the fusion of blockchain with the internet of things (IoT) technologies. The developments in multi-virtual Sensor IoT, homogeneous and heterogeneous multi-system information fusion for BCoT, industrial applications of BCoT has transformed the way digital world work. Ever since the smart devices were introduced, the world has evolved and progressed by making the entire world more dynamic by bringing technology, machines and people together. Smart manufacturing is another emergent sector where BCoT can significantly contribute. Smart manufacturing is basically formed by integrating multifaceted technologies, such as IoT-enabled technologies, service-oriented and cloud manufacturing, blockchain, etc., in various industrial applications. In fact, the IoT, particularly the industrial internet of things (IIoT) are enhancing sensor usage and remarkably contributing to smart manufacturing. This article contributes to the existing knowledge domain by exploring and studying various sensors and proximity sensors in details, customer and product movement, reaction of customers towards sensors and smart technologies based on BCoT, usages and advantages of sorting techniques with regards to the memories of BCoT devices and sensors, a precise measurement system using quick sort for smart manufacturing and future challenges and possibilities.

Keywords: BCoT · Measurement management system · Proximity sensor · Smart manufacturing and sensors

1 Introduction

Blockchain [1, 2] integrated with the internet of things (IoT) [3], i.e. the blockchain of things (BCoT) [4], is revolutionising the Industry 4.0 [5] as well as the emerging Industry 5.0. BCoT has been being employed to multifaceted manufacturing and/or industrial applications, since it provides the necessary supports to create a smart manufacturing system which is highly automated and decentralised with high level of productivity and efficiency.

© ICST Institute for Computer Sciences, Social Informatics and Telecommunications Engineering 2023
Published by Springer Nature Switzerland AG 2023. All Rights Reserved
M. H. Miraz et al. (Eds.): iCETiC 2022, LNICST 463, pp. 29–53, 2023.
https://doi.org/10.1007/978-3-031-25161-0_3

Sensors, a fundamental component of the Internet of Things (IoT), are used in our homes and workplaces being embedded in various smart devices. They are used in different formal and informal infrastructures where digital technologies are used for security purposes or to detect or collect data from any harbingers, for example in industries, shopping centres, hospitals, etc.

Sensors can 'sense' and respond to fluctuations in various aspects of the surrounding environment, such as pressure, light, motion, temperature, etc. These connected devices are capable to output information on the basis of what they detect by sharing data with other connected devices as well as management systems. Since IoT sensors are now widely used there is plenty of room for improvements, which will result in enhanced operational efficiency, reduced cost, enhanced safety measures, across the board automation, etc.

Proximity sensors are mostly applicable in industrial sectors. In this paper, we focused on the improvement of technology which would be more relevant in large clothing stores, hypermarkets, furniture stores or in other centres where there will be a juggernaut of connectivity of prices, commodities and customers. That being said, the proposed measurement management system can be used in many other aspects too.

The smart manufacturing sector is drastically expanding, embracing the emerging technologies. However, utilisation of third-party-based authorisation and centralised industrial networks lead to lower efficiency, lesser flexibility, lower scalability and weaker security. To address these issues, BCoT can play a vital role. In this context, this article introduces an enhanced precise measurement management system utilising BCoT-based smart manufacturing. The proposed measurement system utilises quick sort to easily detect a value within a very short time. It can furnish intuitive solutions for addressing the issues and challenges with regards to the limitations of BCoT-based systems.

2   Smart Manufacturing and Sensors

Sensors have been used in the industries and organisations for a long time. In fact, thermostat was first introduced in the late 1880s while the infrared sensors in the late 1940s. The ability to detect was a need from long ago. Sensors are smaller, slimmer and stretchable, stronger and smarter, more solid, more capable and cheaper.

The invention of the internet of things (IoT) contributed in revolution of multifaceted sensors. Its functionality and delivery of different types of intelligence as well as data by using different types of sensors in the whole network of connected devices is making sensors more efficient and smarter. It offers autonomous functionalities by integrating devices, sensors and communication network together to exchange data and information with each other and boost the efficiency of the whole system. These resulted sensors to be an essential part in smart manufacturing.

Therefore, a novel paradigm of measurement system has been proposed in this article, utilising quick sort, which can be viewed as a potential enabler of wide-ranging use cases scenarios as well as applications.

The following sub-sections gives an account of various sensors commonly used in smart manufacturing [6]:

Temperature Sensor - measures the quantity of the heat energy which lets a physical transformation in temperature to be detected from a specific source and translates the captured data to a user or device. Temperature sensors are widely utilised in freezers, A/C control and similar environmental control systems, agriculture, manufacturing processes, health industry, etc., to maintain the manufacturing process always optimal and to maximise output or production. Sub-categories of temperature sensors include: IC (Semiconductor), resistor temperature detectors (RTD), thermocouples, thermistors and infrared sensors, etc.

Proximity sensors - recognises the presence or absence of any product within range, or the qualities of that product and transform it into signals which can be understood by customers or electronic devices without coming into touch. Proximity sensors are utilised in cars, in the retail business and parking lots such as malls, stadiums airports, etc. Sub-categories of proximity sensors include: inductive, photoelectric, ultrasonic and capacitive sensors are examples of proximity sensors.

Pressure sensors - detect pressure fluctuations and decreases in pressure, which are then translated to an electronic signal. The amount here is determined by the amount of pressure used. Pressure sensors are used in the manufacturing industry, in the upkeeping of indoor water as well as heating systems, etc.

Water quality sensors - detect the water quality. These sensors are utilised in manufacturing, for maintenance of indoor water as well as heating systems, for outdoor water monitoring, etc. Examples of water quality sensors include: total organic carbon sensor, conductivity sensor, chlorine residual sensor, turbidity sensor, pH sensor, oxygen-reduction potential sensor, etc.

Chemical sensors - indicate changes in liquid, find out air chemical changes. Chemical sensors are employed in industrial environmental process control as well as monitoring, intentionally or unintentionally released toxic chemical detection, radioactive and explosive detection, recycling operations at the space stations, pharmaceutical companies and laboratories, etc. Examples of chemical sensors include: Chemical field-effect transistor, Hydrogen sulphide sensor, non-dispersive infrared sensor, electrochemical gas sensor, Zinc oxide nanorod sensor, chemi-resistor, fluorescent chloride sensor, potentiometric sensor, pH glass electrode, etc.

Gas sensors - monitor any changes in quality of the surrounding air and sense the presence of different gases. Gas sensors are utilised for monitoring air quality, oil and gas sectors, toxic or flammable gas detection, monitoring of hazardous gas in coal mines, research in chemical laboratories, manufacturing – pharmaceutical, rubber, plastics, paints and petrochemical, etc. Examples of gas sensors include: carbon dioxide sensor, hydrogen sensor, breathalyzer, nitrogen oxide sensor, ozone monitor, air pollution sensor, electro-chemical gas sensor, carbon monoxide detector, catalytic bead sensor, oxygen sensor, gas detector, hygrometer, etc.

Smoke sensors - detect smoke, i.e. airborne particulates and gases, and its level. Smoke sensors are utilised in HVAC, manufacturing industry, buildings and accommodation safety measures - detect and alarm fire and/or gas incidences. Examples of smoke sensors include: ionisation smoke sensor, optical smoke sensor (photoelectric).

Infrared sensors - detect certain features or characteristics of the surrounding environment by either detecting or emitting infrared radiation. Infrared radiation can be measured by the heat being emitted by the objects. Infrared sensors are used in healthcare, multifaceted IoT projects, smart watches, remote control, smartphones, breath analysis, home appliances, optical communication, measurement of temperature without any physical contact, wearable electronics, infrared vision, etc. Examples of infrared vision include visualising heat leaks in electronics, monitoring blood flow, seeing under layers of paint by art historians, etc.

Level sensors - work out the amount or level of liquids, fluids, or any other substances which flow in a closed or open system. Level sensors are utilised in businesses involving liquid materials, e.g. the recycling industry, the alcohol and juice industry, etc. Level sensors can be used for determination of liquid levels and fuel gauging in closed or open containers, water reservoirs, monitoring of sea level as well as tsunami warning, machine tools, compressors, hydraulic reservoirs, medical equipment, pharmaceutical and beverage processing, etc. Examples of such sensors include: continuous level sensor, point level sensors, etc.

Image sensors - are employed to transform optical images into electronic signals to electronically store or display them. Image sensors are used in digital camera and modules, sonar, thermal imaging devices, radar, medical imaging as well as equipment designed for night vision, biometric devices, media house, etc. In integrated circuits such as charge-coupled device (CCD), in the car industry, CMOS (complementary metal-oxide semiconductor) imagers, in the retail industry, in improved security systems, in IoT industry, these sensors are deployed for collecting data about customers - aiding businesses in getting better insights of the store visitors by identifying the race, gender, age, etc.

Motion detectors - identifies any motion or physical movement in the surrounding area and it converts the motion into electric signals. Motion detectors are highly used in the security industry, particularly for intrusion detection systems and smart cameras with motion-based capture/video recording., Other usages include but not limited to hand dryers, automated sinks/toilet flushers, boom barriers, automatic door control, toll plazas, automatic parking systems, energy management systems (e. g. automated lighting, fan, AC, etc.), and so forth. Examples of motion detectors include: ultrasonic, passive infrared (PIR), microwave, etc.

Accelerometers - gauge the physical acceleration, i.e. the rate of change of velocity per unit time, of an object caused by inertial forces. Accelerometers are used in cellular and media devices, free fall detection, automotive control aa well as detection, tilting, aircraft and aviation industries, vibration measurement, consumer electronics, sports academy (e.g. athletes' behaviour monitoring), industrial and/or construction sites, monitoring driving fleet and so forth. Examples of accelerometers include: hall-effect accelerometers, piezoelectric accelerometers, capacitive accelerometers, etc.

Gyro sensors - measure the angular velocity or rate i.e. speed of rotation around an axis. Gyro sensors monitors the orientation of an object. Gyro sensors are used for the automation of some production processes in automotive navigation systems, cellular and camera devices, robotics control, consumer electronics, game controllers, drone and radio-controlled (RC) helicopter or unmanned aerial vehicle (UAV), vehicle control or advanced driver assistance systems (ADAS), etc. Examples of gyro sensors include: rotary or classical gyroscopes, optical gyroscopes, micro-electro-mechanical systems (MEMS) gyroscopes, vibrating structure gyroscope, etc.

Humidity sensors - similar to the temperature sensors, detect the change in humidity, almost instantaneously. Humidity sensors are used for controlling ventilation, heating and AC systems in the industrial as well as residential domains, such as automobiles, museums, greenhouses, industrial spaces, paint and coatings industries, meteorological stations, hospitals and pharmaceutical companies to safeguard pharmaceuticals, etc.

Optical sensors - measure the physical quantity of light rays and convert it into electrical signal which can be easily read by user or an electronic instrument/device. Optical sensors are used in healthcare, environmental monitoring, energy, pharmaceuticals mining, aerospace, optical fibre communications, digital optical switches, ambient light detection, assembly line part counters, high speed network systems, civil and transportation fields, oil and gas applications, elevator door control and safety systems, etc. Examples of optical sensors include: photo detector, proximity, fibre optics, pyrometer & infrared.

3 Proximity Sensors

The proximity sensor can sense the proximity of an object (e.g. in an automated production line) without touching it. The existence as well as movement information of the objects are captured and then transformed into electrical signals.

Proximity sensors are used in parking lots to indicate parking spaces, consumer electronics, assembly lines (particularly in chemical industry), food industry, etc. On consumer electronic devices, proximity sensors act as capacitive touch switches; for instance, it can be used for detecting whether a phone user is holding it near his/her face. Proximity sensors can also be employed as diffuse sensors such as in washrooms, or even as collision detection sensors for robots.

Proximity sensors are highly utilised in multifaceted industrial and manufacturing applications, such as for detecting parts in conveyor systems, for safety measures, inventory management for object positioning, detection, inspection and counting, etc.

Proximity sensors typically generates electromagnetic fields or emit radiation beams, e.g. infrared rays. In retail industry, such as in a supermarket, proximity sensors can be employed for detecting the movement between any customer and the product the customer is interested in. Notifications of ongoing promotions and offers can then be sent to that particular customer for the products near the respective sensors. On the contrary, unlike the traditional proximity sensors, capacitive proximity sensors are not limited to only metallic targets. They can, in fact, be utilised to detect 'anything' carrying electrical charges.

The following are some features of proximity with regards to increasing lucidity:

- Contactless (ensuring object stays well-conditioned, detecting both versatile metallic as well as non-metallic objects, including powders, liquid and granular)
- Natural by the surface colours of the objects (usually distinguishes any physical changes)

- Usable in humid conditions and wide temperature range usage, contrasting traditional optical detection.
- Cheaper price but longer service life in comparison with other sensors.
- Higher response rates.
- Emit a light beam using high-end photoelectric technology having the ability to detect any sorts of objects (photoelectric).

The selection of the appropriate sensor depends on various factors. For example, for measuring range/distance, the distance (long or short) between the object placed and the sensor, amount of light, possible obstacles, etc. are to be considered.

Proximity sensors can be further categorised in capacitive sensors, inductive sensors, ultrasonic sensors, photoelectric sensors, etc. Inductive sensors are used in short distance applications and suitable for only metals. They are a good choice for harsh environmental conditions; commonly used in industry machineries and automations. Capacitive sensors are also used in short distance applications, primarily for non-metallic as well as metallic objects including powders granular, and liquid. They are used in industry, automations, liquid and moisture, machineries, touch sensing, etc. Capacitive sensors are highly suitable for using in harsh environmental conditions. Photoelectric sensors, on the contrary are for long distance applications, for object with simple surfaces. They are used in distance measurement anemometers for detecting wind speed as well as direction, automation production processes, fluid detection, unmanned aerial vehicles (UAVs) for object monitoring robotics. They are a good fit for harsh environmental conditions except vacuum. Ultrasonic sensors are also for long distance applications, particularly for object with simple/complicated surfaces. They are used in security systems such as surveillance and burglar alarms, item counter, monitoring as well control applications. However, unlike the aforementioned ones, ultrasonic sensors are not a good fit for harsh environmental conditions [7].

Amongst various types of proximity sensors, we opted for capacitive sensors for implementing the proposed measurement application.

Capacitive proximity sensor generates electrostatic fields when any object (conductive/non-conductive - including glass, wood, metals, plastic, water, etc.) reaches the target area, the capacitances of both the plates increase, causing oscillator amplitude gain which generates sensor output switch. Capacitive proximity sensors are highly suited for industrial applications, e.g. production automation machines which count products, pipelines, filling processes, inks, product transfers, etc., composition and pressure, fluid level, non-invasive content detection, moisture control, touch applications and so forth.

4   Customers' Reaction Towards Sensors and Smart Technologies

An IoT device is a device embedded with at least one sensor that connects to and shares data from the sensor(s) with other devices directly or indirectly via a wireless communication protocol, such as through an IoT hub or a smart device including smartphone.

Sensor can be a component of an IoT device, or a stand-alone object (a radio-frequency identification (RFID) which can be read by an RFID reader) which detects changes. Let us consider the case of a smartphone - it uses a number of sensors, such as a timer, accelerometer, global positioning system (GPS) sensor, etc.

Consumer/customer can be indicated as an entity who purchases a product or interacts with a product for the purpose of purchasing it or does both or equivalents. Normally, a consumer/customer makes purchase decisions of a product on the basis of the information available online or at a brick-and-mortar store.

Consumer device or customer device is owned by a consumer/customer which is capable of communicating with IoT devices enhanced with sensors or without sensors.

Retailers provide products for consumers/customers for purchasing regardless of their physical or web presence. A retailer can play a role as a manufacturer of a product or any other person within the distribution chain of the product.

Marketer provides information (coupon or alert) on products to customers. The marketer or the retailer can collect data on consumers and use that data for marketing purposes.

When customers visit brick-and-mortar stores to purchase anything they may seek assistance from anyone with regards to making purchasing decisions of the products. Customers examine the product by picking up the product, reading its label or viewing a review of the product on a website before making a decision to buy (online or offline). IoT devices are located in the supermarkets as well as in the customer devices (such as smartphone, smart glasses, smart watch, etc.) which collects data from customer devices for the retailer or the marketer. On the other hand, the customer's smartphone can determine the location of the person near a product based on a proximity sensor on the product to determine the possibility of interacting with the product.

The retailer or marketer analyses the sensor data immediately after receiving it in order to determine the interactions between the consumer and an IoT device. To map some interactions, specific sensor data may be required to determine that the consumer has performed that specific communication. The received sensor data is checked to see if it matches the specific sensor data mapped to a specific interaction. If it matches, then we know that the interaction has been identified.

In customer navigation tech (e.g. bluetooth low energy (BLE)) or customer devices, machine-learned models use historical information regarding interaction. Each customer device specifies specific data. For any specific customer, input, output and lead scores are counted.

A standard conversion rate can be calculated based on any type of interaction between a product and a customer, such as when a customer purchased a specific product after examining the details, as opposed to other customers who came across the details.

Finding customers' choices, finding best prices for the product by customer, costing determination by retailer for example garments manager or financial advisor, finding average cost or average values of complicated rates or functions, calculating the most appropriate and relevant scores or costs or values after updating the data or getting additional new data with any specific interval of time, finding the probability of the best choice i.e. proximity of the consumer to the product on the basis of previous calculations for predetermination of cost or choice can be performed by any invention represented as machine-useable instructions or computer codes, comprising computer-executable instructions, e.g. program components run by any computer or other form of computing machines, such as bluetooth low energy (BLE), personal data assistants (PDA) or any other handheld devices. Program components, including programs, routines, components, data structures, objects or code accomplish particular tasks or administer particular data types. Multifaceted factors, such as performance expectancy, social influence, effect expectancy, facilitating conditions, price value, habit, motivation, etc., influence the customers to install a retailer's application (app) on their IoT devices enhanced with sensor, to utilise the respective mobile app in a retail store, allowing their location to be utilised for personalised/customised/targeted service rendering and increase demand and facility towards customer.

We can implement the proposed algorithm (i.e. using quicksort in approximate or precise memory of BCoT devices or sensors) in existing different aspects of the inventions which may be applied in a wide range of system configurations, including customer devices, handheld devices, BCoT- based electronics, computers, computing devices, etc.

For example, Qualcomm introduced proximity beacons while Apple released iBeacon (relays three values: minor ID, major ID and unique ID). Both of these products are compatible with the BLE technology stack as well as can be utilised for tracking indoor location.

The program can be used in distributed computing environments. The advantage of this will be performing any work remotely linked through any communications network. Customers will be benefited by using the system as well as retailers or marketer will get smoother sensors or devices.

One of the most important factors in improving the performance of some real-time BCoT applications is transaction time for data collection and sorting. Transaction time is, however, constrained by the computational and communication capabilities of processing computers. To overcome this limitation, we propose an efficient method for sorting massive amounts of data that employs a progressive quality improvement approach.

The use of industrial internet of things (IIoT) networks within the industrial settings, such as smart manufacturing factories, SCADA and ICS, can lead to a disaster or even financial loss if they fail to initiate or perform their function at the proper time. Which shows, we need to use such a program which takes less time within the performance as well as updating blocks. Smoother function or coding is always helpful for any digital devices.

5   Sorting, Usage and Advantages of Utilising Quicksort in the Memories of BCoT Devices and Sensors

Sorting is a widely explored topic in the domain of algorithms. In point of fact, optimised deployment and executions of some algorithms, including quicksort, has been widely adopted. Examples include optimised implementations in Microsoft Visual C++ 6.0 as well as Intel C++ compilers. In Intel compiler, the implementation of Quicksort has been optimised using Hyper- Threaded technology. In many literatures, various fast algorithms have been designed and implemented for processing transactions as well as disk-to-disk sorting. But if we focus on the sorting algorithms' performance on the conventional CPUs, we will see it is administrated by cache slips and instruction enslavements.

Sorting is a relatively common computer operation that converts a set of "unordered" records into an "ordered" sequence of records. The record here can be any type of elements in computer.

Quicksort is one of the most efficient, fastest (as it has the upper hand in the average cases for most inputs), most used, in-place and comparison-based sorting algorithms which is better suited for large data sets. But this sorting algorithm does not demand extra space. Thus, it performs better on Arrays compared to any other sorting.

In this article we have presented an external sorting algorithm grounded on the quicksort approach. The file that needs to be sorted is stored on a disk; only the blocks which are currently needed are fetched into the main memory.

The time complexity of quicksort is $O (n \log n)$ in the best-case scenario, $O (n \log n)$ in the average-case scenario and $O (n^2)$ in the worst-case scenario. It's running time is actually $O (nB\log(nB))$, where B is the block size.

The sorting algorithm is used for information searching. Due to the advantages Quicksort offers, it is widely used for this purpose, particularly when a stable sort is not required.

Quicksort works by splitting a large array of data into smaller sub-arrays. This implies that each iteration works by splitting the input into two components, sorting them, and then recombining them. The whole process can be summarised in three steps: 1) pick, 2) divide and 3) repeat and combine.

When the data to be sorted comprises of many duplicate values, the quicksort can be improved by grouping together all the values which are equal to the pivot to the middle. The quicksort algorithm then needs to be run recursively to sort the values on the left as well as the values on the right.

The principle of divide-and-conquer is the main base on this sorting algorithm. For the advantages it offers, it is used widely for many purposes. Major advantages of it includes: it uses only a small auxiliary stack thus consumes relatively fewer resources during execution, requires only n (log n) time sorting n items, possess a very short inner loop, etc. Quicksort has undergone through comprehensive mathematical analysis – very precise statement regarding performance issues can be made.

To broadly widen scope of the traditional approximate computing, the approximate memory can be leveraged for improving sorting algorithms' performance, but still producing precise results.

There are three classic and popular sorting algorithms that use approximate main memory: mergesort, quicksort as well as radixsort. In fact, the first two algorithms are comparison-based, however, the last one is not. Without the need for precise outputs, simulation results show that quicksort and radixsort can produce a nearly sorted sequence while dropping write latencies on approximate memory by 30% to 40% [8].

Apart from focusing on approximate computing using approximate hardware, a fast sorting algorithm, on the memory system with both approximate as well as precise memory for ensuring precise results, has rather been proposed. A novel algorithmic level execution mechanism on hybrid approximate/precise memory has been implemented, to generate precise results. Specifically, we propose program mechanism in which the approximate memory acts as an accelerator. If the input data is copied to the approximate memory from the precise memory, and then an existing sorting algorithm is performed on the approximate memory, the approximate results are possible to be precise in the precise memory. If the sorting algorithm is able to produce a nearly sorted result on approximate memory, only a lightweight IoT device is required afterwards. As a result, the cost of devices and data copies between approximate memory and precise memory can be compensated through the gain of uploading the sorting algorithm to the approximate hardware. To enhance the performance of precise computing, approximate hardware can additionally be utilised, which widens the application scope of approximate hardware.

Once upon a time, approximate hardware was only used for approximate computing. As a result, we develop and test commonly used sorting algorithms on hybrid storage systems with approximate and precise storage, as well as show system and architectural insights for enabling precise computation on approximate hardware.

Although the system interfaces are to be sensibly redesigned for supporting hybrid approximate/precise main memory, the required hardware modification remains lightweight as well as easily to implementable.

This algorithm is generated for database and data mining applications. We use the texture mapping and mixing capabilities of GPUs which can be implemented as an efficient Bitonic sorting network.

Meanwhile, in order to improve overall sorting performance, we describe an efficient instruction dispatch mechanism and an efficient memory data access pattern in our novel algorithm. Our sorting algorithm has been used to speed up stream mining algorithms as well as join-based queries.

The results show a significant improvement over previous CPU as well as GPU-based sorting algorithms.

6 Using Quicksort in Approximate or Precise Memory of BCoT Devices or Sensors

6.1 Quicksort: Theory and Experiments

6.1.1 Pseudocode

Pseudocode is an effective way to abstracts away the syntax to let us focus on solving the problem in front of us instead of getting bogged down in the exact syntax language. Moreover, it allows us to work on pure programming logic which provides us a chance to simply write in plain English. Therefore, we start with pseudo code.

QuickSort 1 Sort the orders using Quicksort according to the parcel ids.

Input: User will input the number of parcel ids, n, to generate and sort. Users can input the value of variant, *choice*, to choose option 1 - 4 if they wish to see the details of the parcel id and the delivery cost. 1 for just sorting, 2 for printing the unsorted parcels then sorting, 3 for sorting then printing the sorted parcels, 4 for sorting and printing both sorted and unsorted parcels

Output: The algorithm should print out the time taken to perform the sorting. Moreover, it shall print out the sorted or unsorted parcel ids and the corresponding delivery cost that was generated on demand.

```
 1: Declare hash map uset
 2: Declare struct{id, cost} parcel
 3:
 4: function PRINT(p[], n)
 5:     for i = 0 → n − 1 do
 6:         print out serial number i + 1, parcel id and the corresponding cost
 7:     end for
 8: end function
 9:
10: function PARTITION(p[], left, right)
11:     mid ← (left + right)/2
12:     swap((median of left, mid and right), left)
13:     pivot ← p[left].id
14:     i ← left
15:     j ← right
16:     while i < j do
17:         while p[j].id greater or equal to pivot and i less than j do
18:             j−
19:         end while
20:         while p[i].id less than or equal to pivot and i less than j do
```

```
21:            i++
22:         end while
23:         if i < j then
24:            swap(p[i],p[j])
25:         end if
26:      end while
27:      swap(p[left],p[i])
28:      return i
29:  end function
30:
31:  function QUICKSORT(p[], left, right)
32:      if left < right then
33:         pivotIndex ← partition(p, left, right)
34:         QUICKSORT(p, left, pivotIndex − 1)
35:         QUICKSORT(p, pivotIndex + 1, middle)
36:      end if
37:      return
38:  end function
39:
40:  function COUNTSORTTIME(p[], int n)
41:      freq ← system clock cycle frequency
42:      startTime ← current clock cycle counted
43:      QUICKSORT(p, left, right)
44:      endTime ← current clock cycle counted
45:      time ← (startTime − endTime) * 1000000/freq
46:      return time
47:  end function
48:
49:  function MAIN
50:      n ← user input number of parcels
51:      declare parcel p[n]
52:
53:      initialize seed for rand()
54:      initialize seed rd for mersenne_twister_engine
55:      standardize mersenne_twister_engine with rd()
56:      encapsulate engine to function randomLarge()
57:
58:      for i = 0 → n − 1 do
59:         value ← large random integer
60:         while 1 do
61:            it ← traverse uset using an iterator to find value
62:            if it is the end of uset then
63:               p[i].id ← value
64:               break
65:            else
66:               value ← new large random integer
67:               it ← traverse uset using an iterator to find value
68:            end if
69:         end while
70:         p[i].id ← value
71:         p[i].cost ← random double value
72:      end for
73:
74:      display user interface to show options
```

```
75:     choice ← user choose one from options
76:     if choice == 1 then
77:         print out the return value of COUNTSORTTIME(p, n)
78:     end if
79:     if choice == 2 then
80:         PRINT(p,n)
81:         print out the return value of COUNTSORTTIME(p, n)
82:     end if
83:     if choice == 3 then
84:         print out the return value of COUNTSORTTIME(p, n)
85:         PRINT(p,n)
86:     end if
87:     if choice == 4 then
88:         PRINT(p,n)
89:         time ← COUNTSORTTIME(p, n)
90:         PRINT(p,n)
91:         print out the value of time
92:     end if
93:     empty p
94:     return
95: end function
```

6.1.2 Growth Rate

Normally, growth rate refers to how the scale of the algorithm's time complexity and space complexity increase as the scale grows. In addition to predicting the performance of the algorithm, analysing the growth rate helps to classify problems as well as algorithms by difficulty. This is very useful when we compare different algorithms accordingly.

Under normal circumstances, we can analyse the growth rate of the algorithm through two methods: empirical analysis and theoretical analysis [6]. Here we apply the empirical analysis to find the growth rate of the algorithm.

6.1.3 Experimental Data

To test the growth rate of the program using empirical analysis method, we run the program with the following n values: 1000, 3000, 5000, 8000, 100000, 15000, 25000, 35000, 51200, 66000, 86400, 100000, 125000, 150000, 180000, 200000, 250000, 300000, 4000000, 500000, 600000, 700000, 800000, 900000, 1000000.

In order to ensure the accuracy of the data, we adopt the method of taking the average of multiple measurements. For each of them, we will run for ten times and take the average value as the final value.

Tables 1, 2, 3 and 4 below list the measurement particulars for the series of aforementioned experiments:

Table 1. Experiment result from 1000–25000

	1000	3000	5000	8000	10000	15000	25000
Experiment 1	93.5	351.1	598.2	896.3	995.3	1505.0	2989.5
Experiment 2	85.5	349.2	537.6	777.5	1128.6	1496.6	2987.6
Experiment 3	88.2	288.3	541.1	798.1	995.7	1627.4	3550.2
Experiment 4	96.1	312.8	568.3	911.5	1207.3	1396.9	3306.7
Experiment 5	99.6	311.9	538.1	882.6	1134.9	1456.2	3107.6
Experiment 6	95.7	271.7	628.3	788.8	1085.2	1640.7	2860.8
Experiment 7	87.2	289.5	541.4	852.4	1198.3	1505.3	3300.4
Experiment 8	89.1	309.9	562.4	889.1	1067.5	1550.4	3421.5
Experiment 9	84.5	301.2	589.7	873.6	952.2	1589.0	3523.4
Experiment 10	86.2	303.6	601.2	885.4	987.4	998.6	3601.9
Average	90.6	308.9	570.6	855.5	1075.2	1476.6	3265.0

Table 2. Experiment result from 35000–150000

	35000	51200	66000	86400	100000	125000	150000
Experiment 1	4305.9	5592.3	7487.2	10028.9	13214.8	16932.8	19908.0
Experiment 2	4290.6	5166.1	6689.7	9730.2	12551.0	16301.4	18376.2
Experiment 3	4019.6	4984.9	6624.4	10784.8	12790.9	15925.9	20291.9
Experiment 4	4400.7	5380.9	6664.9	10069.0	12761.1	16476.8	19234.9
Experiment 5	4002.5	4810.7	6655.9	9645.5	13457.1	16049.6	20474.8
Experiment 6	4104.4	5243.0	6677.8	10882.4	12999.3	16861.1	19275.0
Experiment 7	4003.3	5067.7	6638.6	9966.0	12852.6	15140.6	20116.7
Experiment 8	4307.1	5101.7	6674.1	10662.9	12633.1	15678.9	19507.6
Experiment 9	4461.1	5376.7	6622.7	10962.3	12845.8	15154.2	18954.7
Experiment 10	4040.4	4976.7	6611.8	10808.6	12562.0	15003.0	19960.8
Average	4193.6	5170.1	6734.7	10354.1	12866.8	15952.4	19610.1

Table 3. Experiment result from 180000–600000

	180000	200000	250000	300000	4000000	500000	600000
Experiment 1	23917.2	26060.3	32352.6	38931.7	51491.6	66087.5	80563.8
Experiment 2	21946.7	27172.8	29758.0	37532.6	48837.0	66646.8	78239.4
Experiment 3	21186.3	25759.9	30055.8	36384.8	50522.0	65820.0	80201.9
Experiment 4	21580.1	26417.3	30379.3	36802.6	50023.3	63413.9	74872.5
Experiment 5	23456.6	26765.9	29505.6	36721.7	52330.6	65212.4	78974.1
Experiment 6	23561.8	27482.3	29859.6	39207.1	48657.6	72475.8	77629.2
Experiment 7	23311.9	26960.4	30555.2	35618.3	53729.0	68441.6	77005.6
Experiment 8	21331.6	26020.5	31193.8	36113.0	50215.1	63275.0	81014.4
Experiment 9	22532.6	27263.7	30975.6	38039.2	49329.2	72554.4	74982.7
Experiment 10	23383.9	25801.6	31620.9	36535.0	49896.3	64280.8	82908.5
Average	22620.9	26570.5	30625.6	37188.6	50503.2	66820.8	78639.2

Table 4. Experiment result from 700000–1000000

	700000	800000	900000	1000000
Experiment 1	92960.4	106881.0	118951.0	135267.0
Experiment 2	95680.8	92260.1	111529.1	127008.5
Experiment 3	94077.4	92694.6	112814.4	126985.8
Experiment 4	85720.6	105417.3	112653.3	129414.8
Experiment 5	92945.2	96946.4	110922.3	133788.7
Experiment 6	87461.9	100097.9	116653.5	138450.3
Experiment 7	93838.2	91980.6	117413.5	127723.6
Experiment 8	89178.0	95847.4	115637.9	133766.2
Experiment 9	90659.1	96326.0	113625.5	140870.8
Experiment 10	87643.1	105245.6	118134.6	126903.4
Average	91016.5	98369.7	114833.5	132017.9

6.1.4 Summary and Graph

Although the rate of growth varies with the configuration of the machine, the trend is generally the same. To better illustrate it, we plot a graph, refer to Fig. 1 below, to show the growth rate:

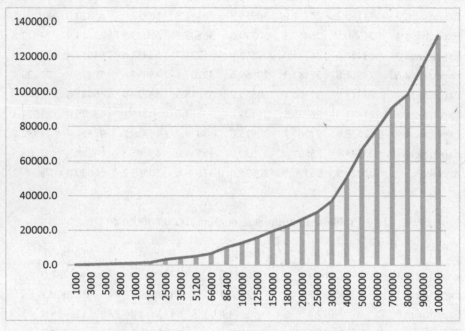

Fig. 1. Relationship between running time and array size.

We already know that the best case of the quicksort is $O(nlogn)$, while the worst case is $O(n^2)$. So, the range where we fit this function is probably from $O(nlogn)$ t $O(nlogn)$.

To find the trend of the average cost, we fit the above function with the following polynomial:

$$y = 362.26x^2 - 4533.2x + 12141$$

Obviously, $4533.2x$ will play an important role in our current data range, so we may first start with growth rate $O(nlogn)$. We try to draw the graphs of $10nlogn$, $nlogn$, $0.1nlogn$ respectively, but they are all larger than the current data. After several attempts, we found the most suitable fitting function which is above our average cost in all values, as shown in Fig. 2 below:

$$y = 0.04nlogn$$

Similarly, we also find another function which is below our average cost in all values, refer to Fig. 3 below.

$$y = 0.01nlogn$$

By definition, we know that the growth rate of this algorithm is $\theta(nlogn)$.

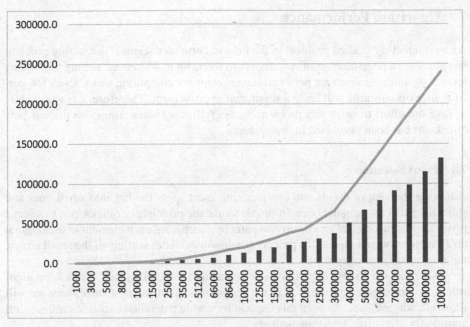

Fig. 2. Average cost and 0.04nlogn.

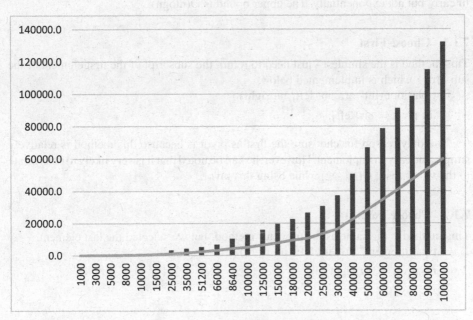

Fig. 3. Average cost and 0.01nlogn.

7   Algorithm Performance

As an intensively studied problem in the field of computer science, the sorting problem has attracted a large number of researchers to focus on it. Moreover, sorting algorithms have a significant impact on performance on complex computing tasks. Even 5% performance optimisation will bring a significant improvement. Therefore, it is worthwhile to take the effort to solve this problem. In the following subsections, we discuss how Quicksort has been optimised in this research.

7.1   Pivot Selection

Adopting the idea of divide and conquer, quicksort splits the big into small ones and splits the small into smaller ones. In simple terms, the principle of quicksort is to select a pivot, divide the original array into two parts by comparing each element in the original array with pivot, and repeat this process continuously. After sorting all the small arrays, the final result is already sorted.

Therefore, the choose of pivot is very important for the efficiency of quicksort algorithm. The pivot strategy we used in the research is the median of three, here we will illustrate why we have choosen this method by giving a detailed explanation to several commonly used pivot selection methods.

However, if we use different pivots, it may enhance the performance of the algorithm linearly but not exponentially. The upper bound is O(nlogn).

7.1.1   Choose First

This method is the simplest - just need to return the subscript of the first element of the sub-array, which is implemented below.

```
int partition(int* arr, int left, int right)

    int pivot = arr[left];
```

The only reason for choosing the first as pivot is because this method is relatively simple and easy to implement. However, it shall be noted that it is very likely to deteriorate to the worst case $[\![O(n)]\!]$ ^2) while using this pivot.

7.1.2   Choose Last

This method is the same as the previous method, but we selected the last element.

```
int partition(int* arr, int left, int right)

    int pivot = arr[right];
```

7.1.3 Randomised Quicksort

Here, we use a random function to randomly generate a number in the array, the variable *left* is the left boundary of the current array, and the variable *right* is the right interface. We use rand()%(right − left) + left) to randomly select.

```
int partition(int* arr, int left, int right)
    swap(arr[rand()%(right − left) + left], arr[left]);
    int pivot = arr[left];
```

The pivot generated by randomisation may help to solve this problem, but at the same time, it should be noted that the random numbers generated by C++ are pseudo-random numbers generated according to algorithms and random seeds, and most of them have some drawbacks.

For example, the random numbers generated by the rand() function in a very short time are the same. In addition, in order to ensure the randomness of random numbers, these algorithms often require a lot of calculations, which will consume a lot of resources and affect our sorting speed.

7.1.4 Median of Three Partitioning

Select the median of the first, last as well as middle element

```
int partition(int* arr, int left, int right)
    int mid = (left + right)/2
    int pivot =
    min(min(max(left, mid), max(mid, right)), max(right, left))
```

Choosing the first or last one may be due to the fact that the array is close to being sorted and deteriorated to an $[O(n)]$ ^2) algorithm. Randomisation generation can also take a lot of time, and the speed of the algorithm is uncertain. Taking the median of the three numbers, it is likely to be able to reduce this situation. We consider this selection approach to be the best choice, amongst the available ones. Therefore, we choose this method for our research.

In fact, there are other improved versions of median of three, such as median of five and median of seven, however, they are essentially the same.

7.2 Further Optimisation

Although the current growth rate of our algorithm is almost satisfactory, we need to note that this is not the best strategy when the range of the array is too large or too small. One way of better implementation may be the STL sort function [9], which is included in the C++ header file <algorithm.h>.

The STL sort function is not just ordinary quicksort. In addition to optimising ordinary quicksort, it also combines insertion sort and heap sort. According to different quantity levels and different situations, the appropriate sorting method can be automatically selected. When the amount of data is large, it will try to use the method of quicksort partition and recursion at first. Once the amount of data after partition is less than a certain threshold, to avoid excessive extra load caused by recursive calls, insertion sort will be used instead [7]. If the recursion level is too deep, there is a tendency for the worst case to occur, and heap sort will be used instead.

So here are other better sorting techniques in different situation.

7.2.1 Switch to Insertion Sort in Small Array

Fast sorting requires constant recursion. When the array is very small, we can use insertion sorting. Insertion sorting is to insert one element at a time on the basis of an already ordered small sequence. When the length of the sequence to be sorted is between 5 and 20, the use of insertion sort at this time can avoid some harmful degeneration situations [8]. It might be faster to use insertion sort in this case.

7.2.2 Switch to Heap Sort When the Recursion is Too Deep

Heap sorting mainly uses a data structure called a heap, also known as a binary heap. This is a sorting strategy based on comparison. The process of putting elements into the heap data structure is called heapify. Through the adjustment of the heap, we complete the final sorting process. It is often used when the amount of data is extremely large [10].

In addition, we also have other ways to optimise. Here is what we can do to further improve the efficiency of the algorithm.

7.2.3 Multiple-Pivot Quicksort

Since 70s of the last century, some researchers have been committed to implementing double-pivot and three-pivot quicksort algorithms. The paper published by Kushagra et al. [11] also talk about the probability of multi pivot quicksort. This quicksort algorithm uses n pivots to divide the original array into n + 1 arrays, which is a further divide-and-conquer algorithm. However, according to the results of Budiman et al. [12], the performance of the multi pivots algorithm have a great relationship with cache performance and it works best when the number of pivots is three in most cases.

7.2.4 Gather Elements with the Same Value

After a partition is over, the elements equal to pivot can be grouped together, and when the next division continues, there is no need to divide the elements equal to pivot again. In this way, by clustering the elements equal to pivot, the number of iterations can be reduced, and the efficiency will be significantly improved [13].

7.2.5 Find Better Pivot Strategy

As we discussed above, a better pivot selection strategy has a decisive influence on the performance of quicksort. It is necessary to choose a better pivot selection scheme to improve the quicksort algorithm.

Apart from these commonly used pivot selection methods mentioned, there are some other pivot selection methods that might be better. In some special cases, for example, when the most elements of the array are sorted except some of them, we can make targeted improvements to pivot selection strategy. Especially, in the field of engineering calculation or graphics calculation, a lot of repetitive work is often required.

7.2.6 Tail Recursion

If a recursive function calls itself at the end of the function, at this time, we can overwrite the current record instead of creating a new one, thereby improving efficiency. For example, the capacity of our code stack is limited. The conventional method can only sort an array of about 50,000. When we use tail recursion, we can effectively increase the maximum sort, double or even triple.

7.2.7 Multithreading and Multiprocessing

Hardware such as memory, CPU, etc. determine the processing speed. The unit that we allocate resources is the thread. Therefore, if we open multiple processes, more resources will be allocated and tasks will be completed faster. The main effect of multithreading is to increase the number of concurrencies.

In addition, we also use multi-threading to improve resource efficiency. Multiple tasks take turns using the CPU.

7.2.8 Efficiency of Quicksort

The complexity of our quicksort is approximately $O(0.04nlogn)$, which has a certain relationship with the implementation of the algorithm and the configuration of the machine [14].

However, no matter what host machine it is running on, the growth rate would always be the same. In this part, we will analysis the complexity of quicksort in best average and worst case to show why our algorithm appears in that way.

For best case, each time partition can separate it to half, so from n to 1 we need do logn times. But for each level, we shall traverse all the elements.

Best: O(Nlogn)

For average case, we assume that partition can happen in n position each with probability $1/n$.

$(\blacksquare(C\_avg \ (0)=0, \ [\!\![\ C]\!\!] \_avg \ (1)=0@C\_avg=\sum\_(s=0)^{(n-1)}$ ▨ $[\![[1/n \ (C\_avg \ (s)+C\_avg \ (n-1-s))]+n-1]\!\!] \ =2n\!\int\_1^n$ ▨ $[\![1/x \ dx]\!\!] \ =2nlogn)\dashv$

Therefore, the complexity of average case is $O(nlogn)$.

Worst: O(N^2)

In the worst case, the array is sorted or the elements in it are all equal, quicksort degenerates into bubble sort. The time complexity of bubble sort is O(n^2) because each element in the array will compare with other elements.

No O(N) Comparison-Based Sorting Algorithm

Suppose we have an array to be sorted which has the size of n. If we want to order it, we need to access each element at least once to know all the information, but we can't use the additional resource on the constraints of comparison-based sorting algorithm [15]. So, we need more actions to achieve the goal of sorting the array.

We carry out the comparison of sorting algorithms in pairs. We can abstract it into a decision tree. we compare the left child node and the right child node in each node. For an array of length n, there are n! combinations of elements. The result of sorted results is one of them. So, we have n! leaves for the decision tree.

Every time we do a sort, we eliminate at most half of the possibilities. We divide all cases where the left subtree is larger than the right subtree into one pile, and divide all cases where the right subtree is larger than the left subtree into another pile. At the beginning we have n! possibilities, and at the end we only have one possibility, which is the sorted array that we want.

Assume we get the final result after k comparisons:

$$⌊1/2⌋ \, ^\wedge k \, n! \leq 1$$
Therefore,
$$k \geq ⌊\log⌋ \, \_2 \, (n!)$$
Because:
$$n! = n*(n-1)*(n-2)*.....*1$$
For $⌊\log⌋ \, \_2 \, (n!)$:
$$O(⌊\log⌋ \, \_2 \, (n!)) \leq O(⌊\log⌋ \, \_2 \, (n^\wedge n)) = O(n \, ⌊\log⌋ \, \_2 \, n)$$

Beyond Comparison-Based Sorting Algorithm

For comparison-based sorting algorithm, it is possible to slightly improve it. For example, we might improve its time complexity from 0.05nlogn to 0.03nlogn. However, it is impossible to improve it from O(nlogn) to O(n) unless we use additional resources.

It is for sure that we cannot create an O(n) comparison-based sorting algorithm, but if we use additional spaces, we do have better techniques. We have briefly introduced them below:

7.2.9 Radix Sort

We divide the maximum value in the array according to the number of digits, and then sort it by units, then by 10, compare each bit, and so on to make it sorted. The data are fetched according to the queue's rule: first in, first out. The time complexity would be O(kn).

7.2.10 Count Sort

The first step of count sort is that we create an auxiliary array to store elements in it. We then traverse the elements in the original array, use the elements in the original array as the index of the count array, and use the number of occurrences of the elements in the original array as the count array element value.

7.2.11 Bucket Sort

As an extended version of counting and sorting, we first group the sorted numbers into several different buckets. Then we use the mapping function to calculate the corresponding mapping value of the elements in the array. When needed, we directly access it through the subscript. It needs $O(n)$ times operation to do the mapping. However, once the mapping is done in advance, the speed can reach $O(1)$ when searching [16, 17].

8 Concluding Discussions

General Beacon devices or bluetooth low energy (BLE) [18] or any IoT sensors [19] uses improvable programs which can be more effective after improving. Retailers, marketers or industrialists can use data or can easily perform any operation using improved programs.

Limitations of the customer devices or IoT sensors are mainly due to software and hardware constraints. These resource constraint devices sometimes do not have enough space or processing power to run various programmes, such as traditional encryption mechanisms, blockchain, etc. Lightweight cryptography, lightweight blockchain of things (BCoT) have thus became emerging research and development fields. However, the level of security compromised for making them light weight remains a concern which needs to be studied further.

Obviously without these customer devices, blockchain, IoT and sensors, we cannot think about dynamic advancement in industrial, agricultural or in any other sectors or significant revolution in the technological world. When all these are combined, including the fusion and blockchain and IoT i.e. BCoT, in smart manufacturing to manufacture incredible inventions, software is also needed to compete with the journey of the combinations of all of the hardware.

This research enhances utilisation of memory in efficient way. More detailed research needs to be conducted in the future to eliminate limitations by focusing on several factors, e.g. better pivot selection, Hoare's partitioning scheme, handling repeated elements, using tail recursion, hybrid with insertion sort, etc.

In this article, a cache-efficient sorting algorithm has been presented which maps to the GPUs. Techniques to further enhance the computational performance have also been put forward. The proposed novel sorting algorithm not only makes comparatively fewer memory accesses but also demonstrates better locality in the patterns of data access. Taking into account the input sequence's sorted nature, if significantly enhances the overall performance.

Our future plan includes to apply the proposed algorithm for other data mining applications particularly, in the domain of smart industry. In addition, we also aim to develop cache-friendly and efficiently algorithms for other types of computations which will eliminate limitations of memory of BCoT devices, sensors and others.

References

1. Al Hussain, A., Emon, M.A., Tanna, T.A., Emon, R.I., Onik, M.M.H.: A systematic literature review of blockchain technology adoption in Bangladesh. Ann. Emerg. Technol. Comput. (AETiC) **6**(1), pp. 1–30 (2022). Print ISSN: 2516-0281, Online ISSN: 2516-029X. https://doi.org/10.33166/AETiC.2022.01.001, http://aetic.theiaer.org/archive/v6/v6n1/p1.html
2. Emon, R.I., et al.: Privacy-preserved secure medical data sharing using hierarchical blockchain at the edge. Ann. Emerg. Technol. Comput. (AETiC) **6**(4), 38–48 (2022). Print ISSN: 2516-0281, Online ISSN: 2516-029X. https://doi.org/10.33166/AETiC.2022.04.005, http://aetic.theiaer.org/archive/v6/v6n4/p5.html
3. Malik, A.D., Jamil, A., Omar, K.A., Abd Wahab, M.H.: Implementation of faulty sensor detection mechanism using data correlation of multivariate sensor readings in smart agriculture. Ann. Emerg. Technol. Comput. (AETiC) **5**(5), 1–9 (2021). Print ISSN: 2516-0281, Online ISSN: 2516-029X. https://doi.org/10.33166/AETiC.2021.05.001, http://aetic.theiaer.org/archive/v5/v5n5/p1.html
4. Liu, A., Khatun, M.S., Liu, H., Miraz, M.H.: Lightweight blockchain of things (BCoT) architecture for enhanced security: a literature review. In: 2021 International Conference on Computing, Networking, Telecommunications & Engineering Sciences Applications (CoNTESA), pp. 25–30. IEEE (2021)
5. Onik, M.M.H., Miraz, M.H., Kim, C.S.: A recruitment and human resource management technique using blockchain technology for industry 4.0. In: Smart Cities Symposium 2018, pp. 1–6. IET (2018)
6. Vaz, R., Shah, V., Sawhney, A., Deolekar, R.: Automated big-O analysis of algorithms. In: 2017 International Conference on Nascent Technologies In Engineering (ICNTE) (2017). https://doi.org/10.1109/icnte.2017.7947882
7. Song, H., Fu, Y., Zhang, L., Peng, H., Liang, H.: Multi-thread quicksort algorithm based on partitioning. J. Comput. Appl. **30**(9), 2374–2378 (2010). https://doi.org/10.3724/sp.j.1087.2010.02374
8. Shaffer, C.: Data Structures and Algorithm Analysis in C++. Dover Publications (2012)
9. Bahig, H.M.: Complexity analysis and performance of double hashing sort algorithm. J. Egypt. Math. Soc. **27**(1), 1–12 (2019). https://doi.org/10.1186/s42787-019-0004-2
10. Li, H., Chen, P., Wang, Y.: Heap sorting based on array sorting. J. Comput. Commun. **05**(12), 57–62 (2017). https://doi.org/10.4236/jcc.2017.512006
11. Kushagra, S., López-Ortiz, A., Qiao, A., Munro, J.: Multi-pivot quicksort: theory and experiments. In: 2014 Proceedings of the Sixteenth Workshop on Algorithm Engineering and Experiments (ALENEX), pp. 47–60 (2013). https://doi.org/10.1137/1.9781611973198.6
12. Budiman, M., Zamzami, E., Rachmawati, D.: Multi-pivot quicksort: an experiment with single, dual, triple, quad, and penta-pivot quicksort algorithms in python. In: IOP Conference Series: Materials Science and Engineering, vol. 180, p. 012051 (2017). https://doi.org/10.1088/1757-899x/180/1/012051
13. Wild, S.: Dual-pivot and beyond: the potential of multiway partitioning in quicksort. IT – Inf. Technol. **60**(3), 173–177 (2018). https://doi.org/10.1515/itit-2018-0012
14. Jadoon: Design and analysis of optimized stooge sort algorithm. Int. J. Innov. Technol. Explor. Eng. **8**(12), 1669–1673 (2019). https://doi.org/10.35940/ijitee.l3167.1081219
15. Bustos, B., Pedreira, O., Brisaboa, N.: A dynamic pivot selection technique for similarity search. In: First International Workshop on Similarity Search and Applications (Sisap 2008) (2008). https://doi.org/10.1109/sisap.2008.12

16. Faujdar, N., Saraswat, S.: The detailed experimental analysis of bucket sort. In: 2017 7Th International Conference on Cloud Computing, Data Science & Engineering - Confluence (2017). https://doi.org/10.1109/confluence.2017.7943114

17. Faujdar, N., Ghrera, S.: Performance evaluation of parallel count sort using GPU computing with CUDA. Indian J. Sci. Technol. **9**(15) (2016). https://doi.org/10.17485/ijst/2016/v9i15/80080

18. Cordiglia, M., Van Belle, J.-P.: Consumer attitudes towards proximity sensors in the South African retail market. In: Proceedings of the 2017 Conference on Information Communication Technology and Society (ICTAS), pp. 1–6 (2017). https://doi.org/10.1109/ICTAS.2017.7920651

19. Miraz, M.H., Ali, M.: Integration of blockchain and IoT: an enhanced security perspective. Ann. Emerg. Technol. Comput. (AETiC) **4**(4), 52–63 (2020). Print ISSN: 2516-0281, Online ISSN: 2516-029X. https://doi.org/10.33166/AETiC.2020.04.006, http://aetic.theiaer.org/archive/v4/v4n4/p6.html

Investigation of the Digitalisation Process of Traditional Businesses and Its Concept for Retail

Waldemar Pfoertsch[1,2](✉) [iD] and Maaruf Ali[2] [iD]

[1] CIIM, Cyprus International Institute of Management, 2107 Aglandjia, Nicosia, Cyprus
waldemar@ciim.ac.cy
[2] Industrial Engineering Department, Canadian Institute of Technology, Tirana, Albania
Maaruf@ieee.org

Abstract. The present state and future evolution of digitalisation of businesses and marketing is seen to be hinged upon the application of the Internet of Things (IoTs). This treatise concentrates on the digital transformative process of how contemporary business operations are being affected in all its scope. The current patterns in e-Business and e-Commerce are identified followed by the phases of the digitalisation process. In spite of some detrimental developments, there is much scope for positivity due to the beneficial effects on marketing from the application of digitalisation. These beneficial effects being dematerialisation and individualisation in the business management. This is also creating a new relationship between the customer and the supplier. The process of digitalisation is also positively impacting marketing. However, the application of information technology brings with it the danger of system failure and cybercrimes. These are active areas for further research among many new emerging research topics.

Keywords: Dematerialization · Digitalization in marketing · e-Business · e-Commerce · GPS · Homo digitalis · Industry 4.0 · IoE · IoT · SoLoMo Mindset

1 Introduction

Knowing how to steer through the current industrial disruptive technologies is critical for the survival of these nascent ventures. To gain an even deeper practical understanding of these transformative technologies, it is essential to look at how they matured in history. Both positive and negative examples need to be studied in history. Negative examples of failures are Nokia, Blackberry and AOL. The classic positive success stories often cited are of Google and Amazon. They are good examples of how far the application of digital transformative technologies can lead small start-ups to multi-billion dollar global industries.

The lay press often uses the terms digitalization and digitization interchangeably. However, they are quite different. Digitization is the process of converting an analogue signal into a digital signal. Whereas digitalization is the application of electronic processing in the industrial process for say automating, capturing and processing information.

M. H. Miraz et al. (Eds.): iCETiC 2022, LNICST 463, pp. 54–66, 2023.
https://doi.org/10.1007/978-3-031-25161-0_4

Digitalization also includes the application of the Internet of Things (IoTs) and the Internet of Everything (IoE). The application of digitization and processing of information by digitization at the point of capture if in the raw analogue format along with all the supporting electronic equipment are all involved in the "digital transformation" of current businesses into the new fully digital business models. Having a fully digitalized business offers many advantages such as the ability to remotely monitor the enterprise and control the whole logistic chain. Digitalization is becoming ever more pervasive covering the spectrum of the economic and political scene [1]. Industry 4.0 is actually the first step towards the full use of Artificial Intelligence (AI), with total collaboration being envisioned between humans and AI sentient beings in Industry 6.0.

2   The Modus Operandi of Digitalization

Having a signal converted into a digital format is merely the first step in the path to digitalization. It is actually the ability for the systems and machines to be able to process the digitally available information and make them operable. This is aided by computer networking technologies meeting the task objectives. This greater flexibility of remote working greatly allows for the expansion of the business model to other applications and markets, leading to more technological innovations. In history, war has shown it to be a major factor for accelerated technological progress. However, similar adverse conditions like the Coronavirus pandemic has had a similar effect particularly in the growth of e-Business and e-Commerce within the span of less than a year. This leap in technology was also seen in its application to healthcare and medical diagnostics. Teleworking increased and changed the pattern of work even after the quarantine period was lifted. Consumers who tried online services like banking and shopping continued to do so afterwards. The effect also spread to communicating with family and workers.

The biggest companies to benefit from all these have been the videoconferencing companies like Zoom and Teams and the online streaming of entertainment video services like Netflix. Live streaming using IP (internet protocol) has overtaken the original live service providers using analogue transmission methods. Currently video on demand (VOD) is preferred by the consumers, as it gives them more control over how they use their personal time.

Wolf and Strohschen [2] define digitilization as: "… when analogue service provision is completely or partially replaced by service provision in a digital, computer manageable model" [2].

Thus digitalization is seen as a facilitator or enabler to modify the business model to provide novel ways of earning income and income generating ventures. The application of new technologies is difficult at first to implement as it often entails a steep learning curve. This is compounded by the fact that these technologies need to be monitored, maintained and adapted to the rapidly changing market condition in order for both the business and the technology to stay viable and useful [3]. What are unique features in a product are now becoming standardized [4]. Moreover, the enterprise-customer relationship is shifting with the enterprise continuing to relinquish ever greater control. The type of customers that retailers face ranges from the emboldened *prosumer* and *digital native* to *Homo Digitalis* (from *Homo Oeconomicus*) [5].

The rapid pace of change is often overlooked by some researchers and its consequent ramifications on e-Business. The time to adopt new technologies continues to decrease. With the invention of telephones, it took around 70 years of its existence before it reached 50% of the household. This is in stark comparison of only a decade for Internet accessibility. This shortening of the timeframe continues to contract to scales of months or weeks. This means industry needs to be more adaptable and responsive to the accelerated pace of change or simply not survive.

Digitization needs to encompass all aspects of the business, that is from the socio-politico-economical interfaces. This is addressed in [6] with a discussion on how employability is affected by digitization and also the changing patterns of consumer demands. This also leads to how the balance and dichotomy between the interplay and interaction between man and machine need to be balanced. There may be cases of difficulty in determining at certain times which component is actually in control [3]. The permeation of digitalization and its ubiquity has led to terms such as megatrend [7, 8] or even gigatrend [9]. As Linden and Wittmer [9] states, "for a development to be considered a gigatrend it must influence all existing megatrends, on all areas of life and this on a global scale while having a half-life period of at least 30 years".

In 1991, it all began with the first homepage at CERN (Conseil Européen pour la Recherche Nucléaire) [10]. The computers were fixed with the ultimate goal being data processing by automated means and application of Enterprise Resource Planning (ERP).

Around 2001 Web 2.0 applications began with the foundations of Cloud Computing and Big Data. Another decade later, in 2011, the term Industry 4.0 was used in Germany. Mobile applications and digitalisation of the industry now became more widespread and mainstream with the full rollout of Industry 4.0 – using existing technologies, infrastructure and new computer networking technologies.

Figure 1, shows the digital transformation in the various fields from the consumer to the industry; Fig. 2 shows the differentiation between external digitalization and internal digitalization; Figs. 3 and 4 show what constitutes Industry 4.0.

2.1 The Evolutionary Steps of Digitalization

Figure 2, clearly delineates between external digitalization and internal digitalization and the evolutionary steps of digitalization. These steps consist of three phases [12, 13] (see Fig. 2). All the stages clearly distinguish between the internal and external digitalization.

First Phase: The Data Processing Fundamentals
The first stage is the deployment of the infrastructure foundation with the networking system [12].

Second Phase: Interconnected Communication and Information Dissemination
This stage carries on from the first phase with the full implementation of networking with external networks. This phase is implemented company-wide [12].

Third Phase: Interconnection of Products and Services
The fourth industrial revolution [14] can only happen with digitalisation. Schlick proffers that we are at the beginning of a new epoch based on cyber-physical systems (CPS).

These are described as "distributed, intelligent objects that are interconnected via Internet technologies" [13]. This phase is seen to be economically disruptive leading to the emergence of new business models and disappearance of old ones.

Fig. 1. Digital transformation: from the personal to the industrial level [11].

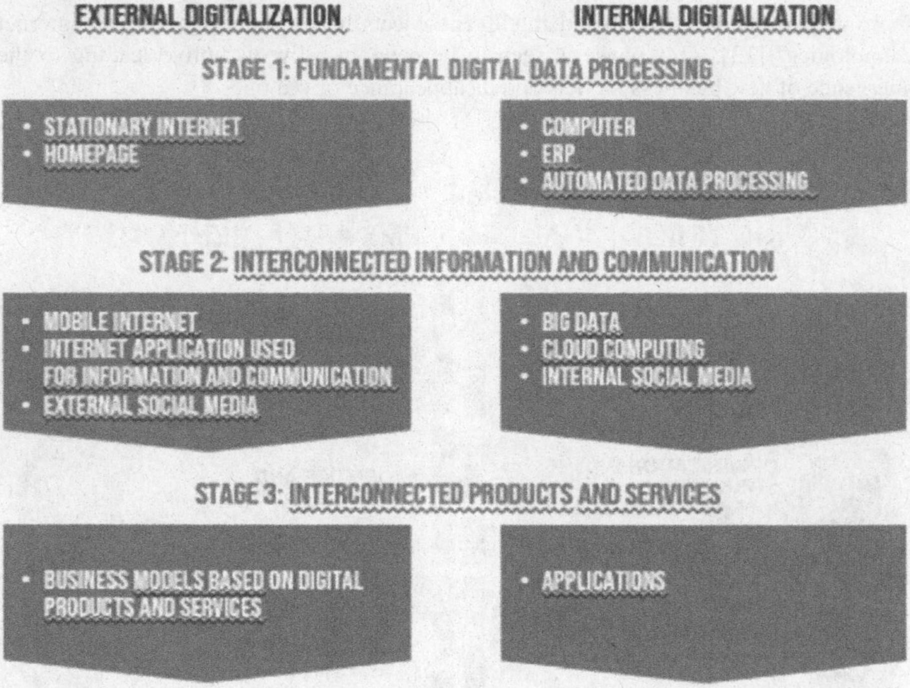

EXTERNAL DIGITALIZATION   **INTERNAL DIGITALIZATION**

STAGE 1: FUNDAMENTAL DIGITAL DATA PROCESSING

- STATIONARY INTERNET
- HOMEPAGE

- COMPUTER
- ERP
- AUTOMATED DATA PROCESSING

STAGE 2: INTERCONNECTED INFORMATION AND COMMUNICATION

- MOBILE INTERNET
- INTERNET APPLICATION USED
  FOR INFORMATION AND COMMUNICATION
- EXTERNAL SOCIAL MEDIA

- BIG DATA
- CLOUD COMPUTING
- INTERNAL SOCIAL MEDIA

STAGE 3: INTERCONNECTED PRODUCTS AND SERVICES

- BUSINESS MODELS BASED ON DIGITAL
  PRODUCTS AND SERVICES

- APPLICATIONS

Fig. 2. The evolutionary steps of digitalization, adapted from [12].

2.2 Industry 4.0

Overall, we are at the verge of Industry 4.0 with all the technologies required present as shown in Fig. 3.

Some firms are already at the third phase [12] with the existence of the *smart factory* and *smart service world*. Figure 4 shows the technologies and related fields of Industry 4.0. However, complete digital transformation is just starting [15] with complete interplay between the digital and physical world still not complete [16]. Global electrical manufacturers are working frantically to achieve complete digital transformation. Siemens for example are using Augmented Reality (AR) and Virtual Reality (VR) with the assistance of Artificial Intelligence (AI) in their products to be competitive.

The consulting agency Pierre Audoin Consultants has found regional differences in the implementation of technology and digitalisation [18]. This study on digital strategy in midsize to large firms [19] was carried out in France, Germany and the UK. The findings showed that 28% was pursuing a company-wide digital strategy, 72% are in the early stages of the digital transformation. However, 69% had a key person for all digitalization projects, while 14% had a Chief Digital Officer (CDO). Most used their Chief Marketing Officer (CMO) or their Chief Information Officer (CIO) in rare cases for digitalisation tasks. This shows how the marketing department must now learn new skills and knowledge in digitalisation. This is why digitalisation is one of the most important factors in its influence in H2H (Human-to-Human) Marketing. Car manufactures have

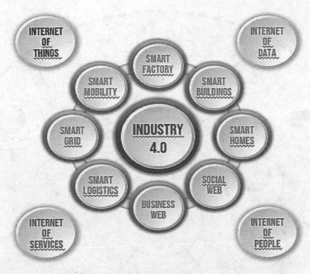

Fig. 3. The Industry 4.0 environment, adapted from [14].

adopted digitalisation more than any other industry. An example is Mercedes Benz with their integrated car assembly line using intelligent networks.

3 The Effect of Digitalization upon Marketing: Dematerialization and Customization of the Value Proposition

While commodities are losing their differentiating factor, the importance of the value proposition is becoming ever pertinent. This trend is growing in many industries such as in B2C (Business-to-Consumer) as well as B2B (Business-to-Business) [4]. Examples include travel agencies offering personalised services through web portals and the prevalence of internet banking. Due to the Internet and the availability comparison websites, the importance of the value proposition is become more critical to the company to survive with their shift to personalisation, service and solution providers [3]. They are the most successful in countering the commoditization tendency. Customers have now become independent information seekers, no longer reliant on the companies as providers of this information.

Customers also participate in customer-to-customer (C2C) interaction, to discuss the suitability of the product before its purchase [20]. Overall, this trend in the growth of individualisation due to digitalisation is depicted in Fig. 5, below.

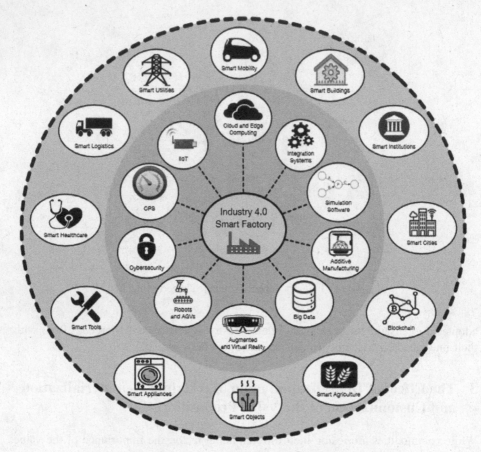

Fig. 4. The technologies and related fields of Industry 4.0 [17].

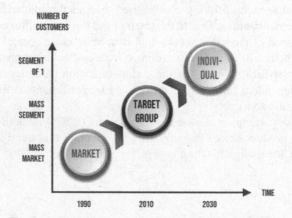

Fig. 5. Individualization as a result of digitalization [21].

The resources to support this need for individualisation is from the cost saving by digitalisation due to the almost zero marginal cost of the digital product.

Digitalisation offers the selling of niche products and also the market entry globally.

Digitalization is also leading towards the product not requiring to be even in physical form, as shown in Fig. 6. In the process of dematerialization, the products and services now only exist as software and apps. Even the value chain is becoming obsolete [22].

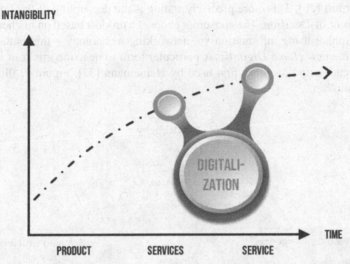

Fig. 6. Digitalization driven dematerialization, adapted from [24].

The consequences of the "sharing economy", further aggravate the dematerialization process [23].

The underlying hardware structure composed of the network enabled elements will also be changed with the proliferative use of Internet of Things (IoT) objects. Land [22] explains that IoT should really be seen as "Internet of Services" and "world machines". Furthermore, for firms operating in this new hardware, they should position themselves as providing software services and not mainly provider of physical products [22].

Dematerialization (conversion of physical share certificates into an electronic form) affects marketing directly. One aim of H2H marketing is to rematerialize some demate-rialization, such as the value proposition. This is seen as helping humans reconnect with the product in the physical realm. This can be achieved using Virtual Reality along with Augmented Reality when showcasing a product that only exists in the digital domain. This has other application such as in training and providing customer services when products are moving more and more into the digital domain.

3.1 The Effect of Digitalization upon Marketing and Customer Behaviour

Consumers today rely more upon each other and opinion forums than on the product manufacturers and producers [20]. This shift in the customer behaviour is made possible with the Information Age and Networking Age. This is because, "Consumers now have real-time, mobile access to data that they had previously relied on brands to provide them with" [3]. Purchasing a product was previously made at the point-of-sale where the good was available by physically travelling to that location. The comparison and final decision being made on-site [25]. The customer in fact now suffers from a surfeit of information being spoilt for choice. The customer behaviour is also monitored and a preference profile built up based on the browsing history, such that selected and personalised information is fed to the customer. Social influence can also steer the purchaser through peer pressure internet forums [26]. This more precisely stating is the decoupling of the Point-of-Sale from the Point-of-Decision. The consumer chooses a product based on his/her needs and then the supplier using information via networking technology – this is the shopping pattern of the new *Homo Digitalis*. A particular term to describe this trait is SoLoMo (Social Location and Mobile), first used by Heinemann [27]. Figure 7, illustrates the SoLoMo mindset.

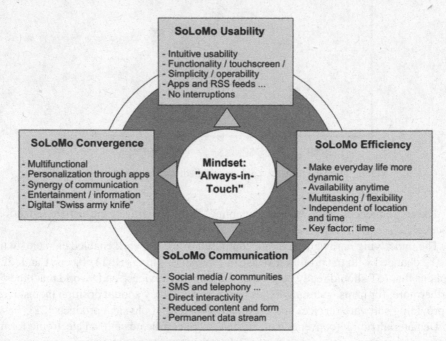

Fig. 7. The SoLoMo Mindset [28].

The acronym SoLoMo perfectly describes the nature of this Homo Digitalis, being rooted around their own internet social network, using localised services whilst being a mobile person – all through their smartphone. Being a socially networked person does mean being influenced more by third party opinions of others [20].

Heinemann [27] in his extensive study distinguishes the mindset of these new generation of *smart natives* as being *Always-in-Touch*, being similar in this respect to those of the *digital natives*, furthermore with a predilection for technology. These are in addition based on these four parameters: *Always-On*; *Always-In-Touch*; *SoLoMo Usability* and *SoLoMo Efficiency* [27]. A fifth trait is also added [27] with that being *SoLoMo*

Communication. This fifth trait can only truly be available if the other four columns are successfully functional.

The SoLoMo Convergence "[…] describes the combination of different functions, contents and channels in a single device" [27].

Modern marketing must be responsive to the new mindset of the consumer. This involves reimagining of the current business models in addition to with the new opportunities given with the use of digitalisation.

After the 2018 data breach by Cambridge Analytica of Facebook data, it has become public knowledge that personal data can be harvested and used unethically, without consent to create user profiles of political leanings and other sensitive information incorporating protected data [29]. The legal laws are still immature regarding these infractions. Traditional companies may view digitalization as ominous [30], however, they may be used [ethically] to gain a better understanding of the consumer and for effective marketing [31].

3.2   The Effect of Digitalization upon Marketing and the Relationship Between the Customer and Supplier

Being sent an unsolicited package with an item that is likely to be accepted is one possibility of the use of personalised information with a better knowledge of the customer [5]. This is only possible with massive gathering of information using Data Analytics and Big Data. For example, Amazon offers a suggestion system without sending unsolicited products. The decision being based on past purchasing history. Etsy also followed a similar route. Spotify started their launch by giving access and a dissemination platform to new musical artists.

The role of the customer has also changed to that of a prosumer with more involvement with the seller and manufacturer of the product. The consumer's views are now taken more into account during the product manufacturing process. The consumer, for example, can be a product tester, lead user and giver of ideas during – a process known as *open innovation* [25]. The consumer can also be involved in the fine tuning of the product to his/her needs to the minutest detail – known as *mass customization* [25].

The consumer can take the role of a co-creator during the manufacturing process, known as *upstream participation*. The opposite scenario is *downstream participation*, where the consumer takes the role of the creator with the company offering a supportive role. Whichever role the consumer takes, the consumer is given the freedom to be an advocate or opponent of the product with reasons [20]. Prosumers can also be employed as low-cost technical consultants by the company [3].

There is, however, the danger of losing control of the whole manufacturing process if too much, unrestricted, unmonitored control is given over to the consumer by the manufacturer. Hence, it is also important to have loyal brand advocates too [2].

Co-creation initially will be a strong product differentiator and a valuable unique selling point when compared against the competition. There does need to be some careful controlled approach so as to avoid any damaging effects of disclosure of trade secrets by the consumer and thus harming the manufacturer.

4 Conclusions

Marketing needs to be aware of the effects of digitalisation and the need to be adaptable in order to survive in this fast-evolving world heading towards Industry 4.0 and beyond. The goal should be for long term viability and success.

The manufacturer must retrain their staff so as to be able to better understand and collaborate with their competent *Homo digitalis*, or prosumers with digital competency skills.

The whole nature of marketing is rapidly changing with digitalisation, especially in terms of the time compression of the product life cycle.

The rapid time to adapt and bring a new improved product to market also carries with it the possibility of the dangers of widespread fast dissemination of negative news through the Internet if a product fails. Thus, the importance of listening to the views of the consumer is even greater now.

The goal must always be to remember that the product being created is for humans and by humans. That is, it is for the benefit of humanity [32].

The Corona virus epidemic of the Spring of 2020 has seen the massive growth of online retailers who took advantage of digitalisation in their whole logistic chain. The lessons need to be learned from this. Even in emerging countries, such as Albania and Vietnam, online sales have started to impact the daily lives of the consumers.

More analysis is needed to systemize the effects in the various markets and situations. To conclude, digitalization is critical for better marketing.

References

1. Ross, J.W., Beath, C.M., Mocker, M.: Designed for Digital: How to Architect Your Business for Sustained Success (Management on the Cutting Edge). MIT Press (2019)
2. Wolf, T., Strohschen, J.-H.: Digitalisierung: definition und reife. Inform.-Spektr. **41**(1), 56–64 (2018). https://doi.org/10.1007/s00287-017-1084-8
3. Ernst & Young: The digitisation of everything: How organisations must adapt to changing consumer behaviour [2011 Report]. https://www.the-digital-insurer.com/wp-content/uploads/2014/04/200-EY_Digitisation_of_everything.pdf. Accessed 14 Aug 2022
4. Schlotmann, R.: Digitalisierung auf mittelständisch: Die Methode "Digitales Wirkungsmanagement". Springer, Heidelberg (2018)
5. Backhaus, K., Paulsen, T.: Vom homo oeconomicus zum homo digitalis – die veränderung der informationsasymmetrien durch die digitalisierung. In: Bruhn, M., Kirchgeorg, M. (eds.) Marketing Weiterdenken: Zukunftspfade für eine marktorientierte Unternehmensführung, pp. 105–122. Springer, Wiesbaden (2018). https://doi.org/10.1007/978-3-658-18538-1_8
6. Precht, R.D.: Jäger, Hirten, Kritiker: Eine Utopie für die digitale Gesellschaft, 6th edn. Goldmann Verlag, München (2020)
7. Naisbitt, J., Naisbitt, N., Philips, D.: High Tech High Touch. Nicholas Brealey Publishing (1999). ISBN-13: 978-1857882551
8. Naisbitt, J.: Der Horizont reicht meist nur bis zum nächsten Wahltag. In: Bundeszentrale für politische Bildung (ed.) Megatrends?. Aus Politik und Zeitgeschichte, vol. 65, no. 31–32, pp. 3–6 (2015). https://www.bpb.de/apuz/209953/der-horizont-reicht-meist-nur-bis-zum-naechsten-wahltag-. Accessed 14 Aug 2022

9. Linden, E., Wittmer, A.: Zukunft Mobilität: Gigatrend Digitalisierung [Monograph] (2018). https://www.alexandria.unisg.ch/253291/. Accessed 14 Aug 2022
10. CERN First Website of the World. http://info.cern.ch/. Accessed 14 Aug 2022
11. Morgan, B. https://www.informatica.com/blogs/12-steps-to-digital-transformation.html. Accessed 14 Aug 2022
12. Saam, M., Viete, S., Schiel, S.: Digitalisierung im Mittelstand: Status Quo, aktuelle Entwicklungen und Herausforderungen, Forschungsprojekt im Auftrag der KfW Bankengruppe, KfW Bankengruppe, Frankfurt (2016). https://ftp.zew.de/pub/zew-docs/gutachten/Digitalisierung-im-Mittelstand.pdf. Accessed 14 Aug 2022
13. Schlick, J., Stephan, P., Zühlke, D.: Produktion 2020: auf dem weg zur 4. industriellen revolution. In: die Fachzeitschrift für Information Management und Consulting, vol. 27, no. 3, pp. 26–34 (2012). https://www.econbiz.de/Record/im-schwerpunkt-industrie-4-0-produktion-2020-auf-dem-weg-zur-4-industriellen-revolution-schlick-jochen/10010019258
14. Kagermann, H., Wahlster, W., Helbig, J.: Deutschlands Zukunft als Produktionsstandort sichern: Umsetzungsempfehlungen für das Zukunftsprojekt Industrie 4.0 (2013). [Report]. https://www.bmbf.de/files/Umsetzungsempfehlungen_Industrie4_0.pdf
15. Lies, J.: Die Digitalisierung der Kommunikation im Mittelstand: Auswirkungen von Marketing 4.0. Springer, Wiesbaden (2017). https://doi.org/10.1007/978-3-658-17365-4
16. Pfeiffer, S.: Industrie 4.0 und die Digitalisierung der Produktion – Hype oder Megatrend? In: Bundeszentrale für politische Bildung (ed.) Megatrends? Aus Politik und Zeitgeschichte, vol. 65, no. 31–32, pp. 6–12 (2015). https://www.bpb.de/apuz/209955/industrie-4-0-und-die-digitalisierung-der-produktion
17. Fernández-Caramés, T.M., Fraga-Lamas, P.: A review on human-centered IoT-connected smart labels for the industry 4.0. IEEE Access 6, 25939–25957 (2018). https://doi.org/10.1109/ACCESS.2018.2833501
18. Teknowlogy: IoT C&SI Survey 2020 [Study report] (2020). https://75572d19-371f-4ade-aeb6-61dbca89834b.filesusr.com/ugd/f21868_2f8ab8213a00460f8777de2057430fb0.pdf
19. Pierre Audoin Consultants: Holistic Customer Experience in the Digital Age: A Trend Study for Germany, France and the UK [Whitepaper] (2015). https://www.pac-online.com/holistic-customer-experience-digital-age
20. Kotler, P., Kartajaya, H., Setiawan, I.: Marketing 4.0—Moving from Traditional to Digital. Wiley, Hoboken (2017)
21. Reinartz, W.: Kundenansprache in zeiten digitaler transformation. In: Bruhn, M., Kirchgeorg, M. (eds.) Marketing Weiterdenken: Zukunftspfade für eine marktorientierte Unternehmensführung, pp. 123–137. Springer, Wiesbaden (2018). https://doi.org/10.1007/978-3-658-18538-1_9
22. Land, K.-H.: Dematerialisierung: die neuverteilung der welt in zeiten der digitalen transformation und die folgen für die arbeitswelt. In: Brüssel, C., Kronenberg, V. (eds.) Von der sozialen zur ökosozialen Marktwirtschaft, pp. 153–166. Springer, Wiesbaden (2018). https://doi.org/10.1007/978-3-658-18818-4_12
23. Frey, A., Trenz, M., Veit, D.: The role of technology for service innovation in sharing economy organizations – a service-dominant logic perspective. In: Proceedings of the 25th European Conference on Information Systems (ECIS), Guimarães, Portugal, 5–10 June 2017, pp. 1885–1901 (2017). https://aisel.aisnet.org/cgi/viewcontent.cgi?article=1120&context=ecis2017_rp
24. Kreutzer, R.T., Land, K.-H.: Digitaler Darwinismus: Der stille Angriff auf Ihr Geschäftsmodell und Ihre Marke, 2nd edn., p. 335. Springer, Wiesbaden (2016). https://doi.org/10.1007/978-3-658-11306-3
25. Heinemann, G., Gaiser, C.W.: SoLoMo – Always-on im Handel: Die soziale, lokale und mobile Zukunft des Omnichannel-Shopping, 3rd edn. Springer, Wiesbaden (2016). https://doi.org/10.1007/978-3-658-13545-4

26. Gehrckens, M., Boersma, T.: Zukunftsvision retail – hat der handel eine daseinsberechtigung? In: Heinemann, G., Haug, K., Gehrckens, M. (eds.) Digitalisierung des Handels mit ePace: Innovative E-Commerce-Geschäftsmodelle unter Timing-Aspekten, pp. 51–76. Springer, Wiesbaden (2013). https://doi.org/10.1007/978-3-658-01300-4_3

27. Heinemann, G.: SoLoMo - Always-on im Handel: Die soziale, lokale und mobile Zukunft des Shopping. Springer, Wiesbaden (2014)

28. Heinemann, G., Gaiser, C.: Social commerce as base factor no. 1 for SoLoMo. In: Heinemann, G., Gaiser, C. (eds.) Social - Local - Mobile. Management for Professionals, pp. 13–54. Springer, Heidelberg (2015). https://doi.org/10.1007/978-3-662-43964-7_2

29. Chan, R.: The Cambridge Analytica whistleblower explains how the firm used Facebook data to sway elections. Business Insider (2019). https://www.businessinsider.in/tech/news/the-cambridge-analytica-whistleblower-explains-how-the-firm-used-facebook-data-to-sway-elections/articleshow/71461113.cms

30. Kozinets, R.V.: Netnography: Redefined. Sage, Los Angeles (2015)

31. LaValle, S., Lesser, E., Shockley, R., Hopkins, M.S., Kruschwitz, N.: Big data, analytics and the path from insights to value. MIT Sloan Manag. Rev. 52(2), 21 (2011). https://sloanreview.mit.edu/article/big-data-analytics-and-the-path-from-insights-to-value/

32. King, K.A.: The Complete Guide to B2B Marketing: New Tactics, Tools, and Techniques to Compete in the Digital Economy. Pearson Education, Upper Saddle River (2015)

Data Integrity for Dynamic Big Data in Cloud Storage: A Comprehensive Review and Critical Issues

Shamiel H. Ibrahim$^{(\boxtimes)}$ ⓘ, Maheyzah Md Siràt ⓘ, and Widad M. M. Elbakri ⓘ

University Technology Malaysia, 81310 Sukudi, JB, Malaysia
{hebshamiel2,mmewidad2}@graduate.utm.my, maheyzah@utm.my

Abstract. Cloud storage services provide vast storage space to solve the bottleneck of the data generated by different big data applications. However, the nature of big data in terms of its massive volume and rapid velocity, needs to be considered when designing data integrity schemes to provide security assurance for data stored in the cloud. The state of the art of data integrity in the cloud includes two primary schemes: (i) Proof of Retrievability (POR) and (ii) Provable Data Possession. Both techniques are designed to achieve the same goal in ensuring data integrity of outsourced data in cloud storage; However, PoR varies from PDP by error-correcting feature to retrieve the damaged outsourced data. This paper focuses on the proof of data retrievability technique (POR) for dynamic data. Dynamic data is defined as data under different update operations. The paper surveys the state of the art data integrity techniques for cloud storage (CS) and previous work on basic requirements for an effective data integrity technique for big data applications. Methods used to provide dynamic PoR are discussed before summarizing the classification of the POR state-of-the-art. The recently proposed techniques and their limitations are also discussed with issues to consider for future POR scheme design.

Keywords: Cloud computing · Cloud storage · Data integrity · Dynamic data update · Proof of data possession · Proof of data retrievability

1 Introduction

The Cloud computing (CC) model has led a new era of internet-based computing models that provide flexible, on-demand, and elastic capabilities. The most recent cloud survey shows that 94% of large enterprises utilize at least one cloud service [1]. This is largely due to the evolutionary change that cloud computing brings to data storage concepts; specifically shift from traditional server-attached storage to network-based distributed storage. In addition, the covid-19 pandemic has also contributed to accelerating cloud usage; surpassing expectation in cloud adoption [1]. Applications that are provided as services via the Internet as well as the hardware and software used in data centers to render such services are referred to as Cloud Computing [2]. NIST defined cloud

© ICST Institute for Computer Sciences, Social Informatics and Telecommunications Engineering 2023
Published by Springer Nature Switzerland AG 2023. All Rights Reserved
M. H. Miraz et al. (Eds.): iCETiC 2022, LNICST 463, pp. 67–81, 2023.
https://doi.org/10.1007/978-3-031-25161-0_5

computing model as a model for providing on-demand network access to a shared pool of customizable computing resources (e.g. Services, networks, servers, storage, and applications) that are supplied and released rapidly with minimal management effort or service provider engagement. NIST cloud computing model is composed of three service models (Software as a service (SaaS), Platform as a service (PaaS), and Infrastructure as a service (IaaS), four deployment models (Public, Private, Hybrid, and community cloud) and five essential characteristics (on-demand self-service, ubiquitous network access, measured services, rapid elasticity and location independent resource pooling) as depicted in Fig. 1.

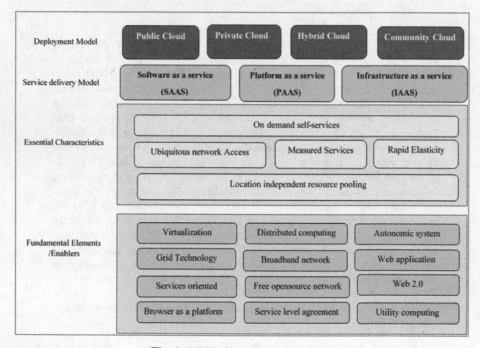

Fig. 1. NIST cloud computing model

2   Data Security Issues in Cloud Storage

Cloud computing provides advantages and benefits over the traditional computing model in terms of convenient commuting, data storage and backup, disaster recovery, and cost-effectiveness [3]. These attractive features support the growing demand for cloud storage services. The storage in the cloud consist of thousands of servers and storage devices joined together with supplied and distributed systems and other middleware to enable cloud service providers to offer cloud storage services to the end users. By adopting cloud storage services, enterprises can improve and expedite operating mode by providing on-demand and elastic data storage resources [4]. Despite its valuable characteristics, not all businesses favor shifting to the cloud, given that the adoption of cloud computing is restrained by several issues such as vendor lock-in, interoperability, reliability, data deletion assurance, and most important, data security and privacy [5]. When considering the shift to cloud storage enterprises' data security is the primary concern. The absence of efficient security practices can lead to unforeseen data breaches such as data leakage due to unauthorized access to cloud data storage. Due to concerns with risk of data leaks in cloud computing, pertinent studies have established relationship between the use of cloud computing and the number of data breach incidents perpetrated by attackers [6]. Figure 2, summarizes the security issues in cloud computing platform [7].

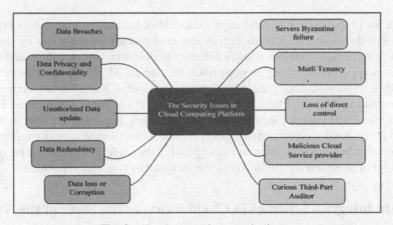

Fig. 2. Cloud computing security issues

Data security in cloud storage has gained considerable attention in academia and in the industry in recent years. So far, concerted scientific research efforts have been aimed at providing methods to guarantee the security and safety of data stored in the cloud [8].

NIST defines three major security requirements for information and information systems: confidentiality, Integrity, and Availability [9]. Data integrity is defined by NIST as an assurance that the data and programs are updated only with authentication and in an authorized manner. Therefore, data integrity techniques protect against unauthorized data alteration or deletion by assuring non-repudiation and validity. In contrast, loss of integrity is defined as an illegal alteration or deletion of data [10].

Data breach happens when sensitive information is exposed to an unauthorized party intentionally or unintentionally [6]. Several incidents of data breach in cloud computing have happened in recent history. For instance, a security breach at Dropbox (www.dropbox.com) was reported to have caused leakage of 68 million user accounts. Likewise, a database failure at Salesforce was reported to result in permanent data loss [11]. Another incident exposed more than 49 million user accounts in the AWS database. Instagram "influencers" and celebrities with large followers were targeted in the attack. Phone numbers, email addresses, profile images, and country locations were obtained during the incident. When the breach was found, it was revealed that the database had been accessible for at least 72 h without a password [12].

Theft of data from a cloud customer's system may occur when an employee acts maliciously; exploiting a configuration error to steal the login credentials of susceptible accounts and access their cloud infrastructure. Approximately 106 million credit card applications, including the names, addresses, and phone numbers of the applicants, were leaked by a former Amazon employee in 2019 [13]. Equifax, one of the three leading credit reporting companies in the US, revealed a compromise in September 2017; leading to a data breach that compromised the personal information of over 148 million Americans whose sensitive and confidential data such as names, birth dates, SSNs, residences, phone numbers, and driver's license numbers. In addition, over 209,000 credit cards were revealed. The magnitude the breach and severity were unparalleled [6].

Data loss may occur due to different reasons. For instance, cloud servers can lose clients' data due to internal reasons such as administrative errors, malicious insiders and hackers' invasions, or external reasons like natural disasters, power failure, and media damage. A typical example is an occurrence on August 31, 2019, when an Amazon AWS US-EAST-1 data center in North Virginia experienced power failure, on restoring the power, some Amazon Elastic compute cloud (EC2) instances and Amazon Elastic Block Store (EBS) volumes incurred hardware damages that led to inability to restore data [14]. The cloud servers can maliciously remove stored data to save storage space or gain economic benefits and generate a valid proof of data safety by reserving previously valid proof or intermediate proof to preserve its quality-of-service reputation.

3   Data Integrity Schemes in Cloud Storage- the State of the Art

The cloud storage model includes two main entities. The data owners (clients) who want to store their data in the cloud, and the cloud storage servers (CSS) or cloud servers (CS), which represent cloud service providers that own broad storage capabilities that are offered to the clients as paid services according to usage [15]. Data in cloud storage could be subjected to different types of security attacks due to resource sharing in the cloud storage model. Hence, data owners need to perform regular integrity checks without downloading the whole data or revealing its content since they do not completely trust the service providers. Several criteria must be considered in the integrity check techniques. In general, the integrity verification method must have a low communication complexity since the primary purpose is to avoid downloading a large chunk of the file to test its extractability. Besides, the protocol's storage overhead must be reasonable since significant server overhead would result in high-cost. Lastly, the integrity verification procedure must have minimal computational cost both for the data owner (who is likely to possess a lightweight device) and the server (whose computation work could also be expensive for the Data owner).

In providing data integrity in the cloud computing model, researchers have introduced two major techniques: Proof of Data Possession (PDP) [16] and Proof of Data Retrievability (POR) [17]. In contrast to the traditional methods that require the possession of entire data files to check the integrity of data, these techniques were established to check the integrity of data without downloading the whole data files from remote servers. Basically, the integrity check protocol executed between the Data owner (Verifier) and the Cloud storage server (Prover) as depicted in Fig. 3, is composed of three main phases:

- **Setup phase:** Before outsourcing the data files, the data owner (Verifier) establishes the auditing protocol by specifying its parameters and pre-processes the files to produce a piece of authentication data called tags or sentinels that are saved stored locally.
- **Challenge/Response Phase:** The data owner (Verifier) generates a challenge request and sends it to the cloud storage server (Prover), asking it to prove the integrity of the remotely stored data files. In turn, the cloud server (Prover) responds by generating the required proof.
- **Verification phase:** This process requires the verifier to check and verify the provided proof without holding the data files (blockless verification). Moreover, the cloud storage server (Prover) should be able to generate the proof without interfering with the content of the original data files (privacy-preserving).

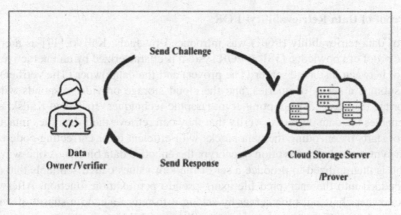

Fig. 3. Data integrity checking- Basic protocol

3.1 Proof of Data Possession-PDP

Many researchers have investigated integrity verification issues in the era of outsourced data storage, providing different schemes. Proposed the proof of data possession (PDP) technique. The scheme is established in the pre-processing phase, where the data owner divides the file into blocks of size 4KB each and generates an RSA alike tag for each file block. After utilizing the homomorphic property of RSA to generate a homomorphic verifiable tag (HVT), the data owner can combine the generated tags into a single value stored locally before sending the data file to the cloud server. Later, the client challenges the server to check data file availability by sending a random challenge against a randomly selected block index. The server responds to the challenge and provides proof of possession for the queried blocks and the corresponding tags. PDP is composed of two stages, setup and challenge phases, described as follows:

- **Setup Phase.** The client runs $KeyGen(1^k)$ to generate both public and private keys (pk, ask) as well as $TagBlock(pk, sk, m)$ to generate block tag $Tm = h((v||i).g^m)^d \, modN)$. The clients outsource the data file F along with sk and $(T_{m1} \ldots\ldots T_{mn})$ to the cloud server.
- **Challenge Phase.** The client generates a challenge chal and requests the server to prove data possession for a subset of blocks in the file accordingly; the server runs $GenProof(pk, F, chal)$ operation to generate the proof of data possession V; lastly, the client verifies the correctness of the provided proof by running $CheckProof(pk, sk, chal, V)$ operation, to output Success or Failure.

PDP protocol gives a probabilistic assurance that the server possesses the clients' data by checking a random subset of stored data. However, the scheme employs RSA-based modular operations for tag generation and integrity verification which entails a considerable computation time at the client and the cloud server-side; a problem for large-sized data files. Besides, the scheme is introduced for static data in private verification mode only and does not consider privacy-preserving issue [17].

3.2 Proof of Data Retrievability- POR

Proof of data retrievability (POR) was introduced by Juels, Kaliski [17] as a crypto-graphic proof of knowledge [18]. A POR system is characterized by an interactive POR protocol between a storage server (The prover) and the data owner (The verifier). The client submits a series of queries, and the cloud storage provider responds with the appropriate responses. By adopting cryptographic techniques, Juels and Kaliski's pro-tocol enables the data owners to verify that they can retrieve their data files intact. The protocol starts by encoding the data blocks with efficient error correcting code before using a symmetric key encryption to encrypt the encoded data blocks. A one-way hash function is then utilized to produce a set of random values called sentinels that are to be embedded into the encrypted file using pseudo permutation function. Afterwards, the data owner challenges the server by asking it to return a certain subset of sentinel in encrypted data. Since the sentinels are indistinguishable from the server, it will be difficult to return its value if the file is corrupted or modified. However, POR itself does not protect data from corruption or loss. It only reveals data corruption or tampering and works with file robustness techniques to strengthen file availability by utilizing error-correcting code. The initial POR scheme which is designed for static archived storage with a fixed number of verification challenges does not consider the case of dynamic data updates. Although, this scheme is secure, however, the permutation of the file blocks to secure sentinels' positions conflicts with I/O sequential performance since sequential blocks in the original file are not in the same place in the resulting file after permutation; thereby limiting the possibility of extending the scheme to support dynamic update operation [7].

4 Public Data Integrity Techniques

Public integrity verification refers to the process of conduct data integrity verification by a party other than the data owner. According to the public model of [18], the scheme involves three entities: Data owner (DO), Cloud service provider (CSP), and Third-Party Auditor (TPA). The integrity checking process is delegated to the TPA who owns the efficient facilities to conduct such verification on behalf of the data owner. Figure 4 depicts the processes followed in a public data integrity audit, consisting of the same phases as the basic auditing technique but with the challenge generated and verified by a third-party auditor rather than the data owner. The scheme proposed by Shacham and Waters [18] introduced the first public data integrity technique that utilizes BLS signature [19] to verify the cloud server response with bilinear pairing function. However, the scheme results in high computational time on the verifier side. [19] Introduced another POR scheme that supports public verifiability by utilizing the independent third-party auditor (TPA), who is well-equipped with the suitable computing resource to challenge CSP and conduct a regular integrity check. However, the scheme does not address the data privacy issue.

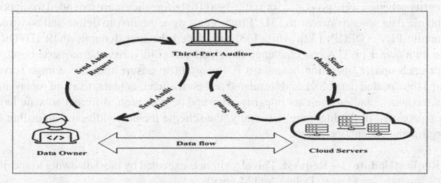

Fig. 4. Public data integrity

[20] Occupy a ring signature to generate an integrity verification token and hide the user's identity. However, since the scheme uses the bilinear pairing to verify the correctness of the signature, its computational cost is relatively high. Similarly, [21] proposed a public auditing method that avoids pairing operations by utilizing homomorphic MAC for tag generation. The scheme preserves the data privacy with blind file blocks with random values, however, the scheme provides for static data only. [22] Proposed a public data integrity technique using BLS-HVT to generate tags that ignores the privacy-preserving issues in the presence of TPA. Different public data integrity techniques abound in the literature using different advanced technique such as Blockchain [23], pairing free [24],and Homomorphic-based signature [25]. To design an efficient public data integrity protocol, preserving data privacy must be considered since both cloud service providers and TPA are not fully trusted despite utilizing different cryptographic techniques such as symmetric encryption [26], Homomorphic encryption [27], data blind techniques [28].

5 Data Integrity Schemes for Dynamic Data

Big data applications often require data upgrades. Given that the contents of many big data applications are dynamic and often updated, it is critical for a cloud security mechanism, such as a public auditing scheme, to support dynamic data effectively [29]. After sending the data to the cloud storage, the data owner may need to apply different update operations for many datasets like social networks, business transactions, and electronic health records. To propose data integrity techniques for dynamic data, the scheme needs to meet the same security guarantees (existence, consistency, and the ability to retrieve the data) for content that can undergo an unlimited number of (legal) alterations. Proofs of integrity techniques are mutual protocols that allow a verifier to validate the consistent existence and availability of data stored in an untrustworthy storage source like cloud storage. According to Juels and Kaliski, developing a PoR method that allows efficient updates is a central open problem [30]. The earliest data integrity schemes were proposed for static data [16] before they were extended to support dynamic data update operations [31]. Erway et al. were the first to define and construct dynamic PDP- (DPDP) [32], while [33] introduced the first dynamic POR (DPOR). The data owner or TPA can challenge the cloud server to verify the requested update after each update operation because it is important to ensure that the storage server keeps the updated data block and its related authentication metadata, to avoid replay and replace attack, and ensure data integrity after update operation, different scheme have been proposed in the literature. Generally, the scheme include additional algorithm to perfume the update operations:

- **RequestUpdate ()→ Request.** This algorithm is executed by the data owner to specify the update type (Insert, Delete, and Modify).
- **Update ()→ Updated Data Block.** This algorithm is executed by the Cloud server taking the encoded file and its related authentication data and the update request as input to produce the update file and its signature while showing the proof of the update as an output.
- **VerifyUpdate ()→ True/False.** This algorithm runs by the TPA or the data owner. It takes the public key, the update operation, and the proof of update to output True or False.

To implement dynamic update operations, different authenticated data structures (ADS) are used to ensure the integrity and freshness of the data block after each update operation. The existing literature reveal different scheme that utilizes the authenticated data structure such as the Merkle Hash tree (MHT) [34], Skip list [35], oblivious RAM [36].

6 Proof of Data Possession for Dynamic Data

To support dynamic data updates operations [37] proposed an improvement for the scheme PDP to support integrity verification for dynamic data updates, reducing the computation cost by symmetric key operation for both the Setup and Verification steps, they enables the data owner to calculate a fixed number of possession verification tokens before outsourcing the data file using a pseudo-random function and pseudo-random permutation to generate a random token for randomly selected indexes. As an advanced PDP for dynamic data, different techniques utilize different methods to provide data integrity assurance in cloud storage. [27] used algebraic signature for authentication tag generation, however, less formal security analysis is performed on algebaric signature so far, whereas [38] used Boneh, Lynn, and Shacham (BLS) signature [39]. Also, [22] proposed a public auditing protocol based on BLS signature to generate a homomorphic verifiable authenticator (BLS-HVA). The scheme utilized doubly-linked info table to support dynamic data update operation. However, the scheme entails considerable computation due to pairing operation in verification phase. Besides, the scheme does

Table 1. Data integrity techniques- the state of the art

No	Scheme	Public	Dynamic	Privacy preserving	Tag	Limitations
1	[39]	No	Yes	Yes	Hash Function	• Restricted no of queries • Partially update operation • Probabilistic integrity assurance, because tags are generated to a subgroup of the tags
2	[43]	No	Yes	No	HVT-RSA	• Does not support privacy-preserving auditing on user's outsourced data
3	[44]	No	No	No	HVT-RSA	• For static data only
4	[24]	Yes	Yes	No	BLS-HVA	• The scheme does not provide privacy-preserving and recovery techniques
5	[42]	Yes	Yes	No	BLS	• The scheme does not provide privacy-preserving and recovery techniques

not consider keeping the privacy of data in the presence of TPA. Likewise, [40] proposed a public dynamic auditing scheme with fair arbitration for cloud storage. The scheme which considers the case of dishonest data owner utilizes BLS signature for tag generation (Table 1).

7 Proof of Data Retrievability for Dynamic Data

To provide proof of data retrievability for dynamic data, [43] introduced a dynamic POR based on BLS signature for tag generation and an improved authenticated data structure based on B+ tree of order three, Merkle Hash tree (MHT) and BLS called Merkle B+ tree (CMBT). The scheme achieves $O(logn)$ worst-case running time. [44] Suggest a practical dynamic POR scheme using the Merkle Hash tree to offer storage authentication since cn erasure-coded needs to be updated in any update block's operation. Besides, the scheme delays the updates of cn parity blocks upon writes. Rather, the client places the newly updated block into an erasure-coded log structure. The scheme, is however introduced for private auditing mode, and does not provide a privacy preserving technique. By using Oblivious Ram (ORAM) technique while utilizing minimum bandwidth regenerating codes (MBR), [45] proposed proof of retrievability with BLS signature for tag generation and bilinear pairing for verification. The scheme was introduced for static data and does not consider the data update operation. Sengupta and Ruj [46] proposed a public verifiable POR based on the storage structure of [44] that utilizes homomorphic hashing to generate another hierarchical storage to eliminate the cost of reading and writing at the data owner's side. The proposed scheme highlights the solution to the data update problem in POR data integrity model. To provide the proof of retrievability, data should be encoded with any of data recovery technique such as error correction code. In case of dynamic POR, the owner of data needs to apply different update operations over the already encoded data. Therefore, all codes related to the updated block should be updated. Besides, data authentication meta-data needs to be recalculated as well, which entails a considerable computational cost. To overcome this limitation, the encoded copy (C) is not updated for each write operation (insertion, deletion or modification). Instead, it is updated (or rebuilt) only after enough of the data blocks has been updated.

8 Issues Proof of Data Retrievability

Generally, three major issues need to be addressed when proposing a POR scheme to ensure data integrity in cloud storage. First, the security of the tag generation algorithm; the proposed technique must provide a secure integrity scheme that resists replay, replace and tag forgery attacks. The second issue is data disclosure by the cloud service provider or TPA during the auditing process. Since a enormous volume of outsourced data and the data owner's constrained computing capabilities make it difficult to evaluate and check the security services in the cloud by the data owners in their own [47]. To introduce the third party to audit the integrity of the cloud services the following two major requirements must be satisfied in order to introduce a third party auditor (TPA) securely, first the third-party auditor (TPA) should be able to audit cloud data storage effectively without requesting a local copy of the data and shouldn't place an extra online strain on cloud users. Second the third-party auditing procedure should not result in any new privacy risks for users' data. The third issue is the increased computational cost of the data integrity process for data update operations; since big data and its applications in the cloud are constantly expanding and changing, the computational and communication cost should be in lower bound in a way that does not affect the security requirements of the proposed data integrity technique, the proposed technique should adopt signature techniques with small key and signature size to reduces the storage space at both data owner and cloud server side.

9 Conclusion

Because of the rise of cloud computing, many bigdata applications are migrating their large data from local to cloud in order to take advantage of the easy and flexible services offered by a CSS, the data owners on the other hand, do not totally trust the cloud storage since they lack direct control over their large data. Data integrity techniques are gaining popularity since it is a necessary prerequisite for ensuring that consumers can trust a CS. There has been a lot of study done on data integrity techniques thus far. Private auditing and public auditing are the two types of schemes, and the literature emphasizes on the latter since it relieves resource-constrained users of a hefty burden. The goal of public data integrity is to allow users or TPAs to verify the integrity of data in CSS with little burden. The idea and system model of data integrity techniques are introduced in this study. Furthermore, a clear discussions are provided from dynamic data integrity techniques and progressive categorization of the data integrity methods depending on the mode of integrity services (PDP) and (POR) is offered focusing on POR for dynamic data. Furthermore, certain major issues and the accompanying technological methods are discovered. Finally, we explore open difficulties and challenges in order to provide some useful suggestions for future research (Table 2).

Table 2. Public dynamic proof of data retrievability

No	Scheme	Data Recovery	Tag	ADS	Limitation
1	[21]	RS Code	BLS	MHT	- Using the classic MHT construction cause an efficiency problem
2	[50]	ECC	Hash-compress and sign (HCS)	Range based -Rb23 Tree	- Huge computation overhead on server-side to rebalance 23RB TREE

(*continued*)

Table 2. (*continued*)

No	Scheme	Data Recovery	Tag	ADS	Limitation
3	[51]	RS Code	BLS-HA	MHT	- High computation cost at the verifier side due to pairing operation in BLS
4	[46]	Erasure code	MAC-based tag	MHT	- Public auditing is not supports - High computation cost due to use of locally decodable codes and Oblivious RAM
5	[52]	RS Code	HA	MHT	- Does not provide privacy-preserving
6	[33]	NC	(ASBB) Based	rb23Tree	- Privacy-preserving not supported
7	[48]	Erasure code	Homomorphic Hash	multi-level hierarchical MHT	- Privacy-preserving is not supported
8	[54]	Information Dispersal Algorithm	BLS -HA	MPHT Multiple Hash tree	- Only modify update operation is supported
9	[52]	NA	BLS-HA	IHT	- High computation cost at the verifier side due to pairing operation in BLS. Not specify data recovery

References

1. State of the Cloud Report | Flexera: State of the Cloud Report (2022). https://www.flexera.com/about-us/press-center/flexera-releases-2021-state-of-the-cloud-report#:~:text=61%20percent%20overall%20plan%20to,a%20centralized%20approach%20to%20cloud. Accessed 9 Mar 2021
2. Fox, A., Griffith, R., Joseph, A., Katz, R., Konwinski, A., Lee, G., et al.: Above the clouds: a Berkeley view of cloud computing. Dept. Electrical Eng. Comput. Sci. Univ. California, Berkeley, Rep. UCB/EECS, **28**(13) (2009)
3. Liu, A., Yu, T.: Overview of cloud storage and architecture. Int. J. Sci. Technol. Res. (2018)
4. Marks EA, Lozano B. Executive's guide to cloud computing. John Wiley and Sons; 2010
5. Takabi, H., Joshi, J.B., Ahn, G.-J.: Security and privacy challenges in cloud computing environments. IEEE Secur. Priv. **6**, 24–31 (2010)

6. Sampson, D., Chowdhury, M.M.: The growing security concerns of cloud computing. In: 2021 IEEE International Conference on Electro Information Technology (EIT), pp. 050–5. IEEE (2021)
7. Tan, C.B., Hijazi, M.H.A., Lim, Y., Gani, A.: VIP2_A survey on proof of retrievability for cloud data integrity and availability: cloud storage state-of-the-art, issues, solutions and future trends. J. Netw. Comput. Appl. **110**, 75–86 (2018). https://doi.org/10.1016/j.jnca.2018.03.017
8. Taneja, D., Tyagi, S.: Information security in cloud computing: a systematic literature review and analysis. Int. J. Sci. Eng. Technol. **6**(1), 50–55 (2017)
9. FIPS P. 199 Standards for security categorization of federal information and information systems. Computer Security Division, NIST (2004)
10. Stallings, W., Brown, L., Bauer, M.D., Howard, M.: Computer Security: Principles and Practice. Pearson Upper Saddle River, Hoboken (2012)
11. Sharwood, S.: Salesforce.com crash caused DATA LOSS (2016). https://www.theregister.com/2016/05/13/salesforcecom_crash_caused_data_loss/. Accessed 02 Mar 2021
12. Chaturvedi, A., Bureau, E.: Instagram data breach trail leads to Chtrbox (2019). Accessed 31 May 2022
13. EPIC: Equifax Data Breach. https://archive.epic.org/privacy/data-breach/equifax/. Accessed 03 Apr 2022
14. Peng, S., Zhao, L., Al-Dubai, A.Y., Zomaya, A.Y., Hu, J., Min, G.Y., et al.: Secure lightweight stream data outsourcing for internet of things. IEEE Internet Things J. **8**(13), 10815–10829 (2021). https://doi.org/10.1109/jiot.2021.3050732
15. Odun-Ayo, I., Ajayi, O., Akanle, B., Ahuja ,R.: An overview of data storage in cloud computing. In: International Conference on Next Generation Computing and Information Systems (ICNGCIS). IEEE (2017)
16. Ateniese, G., Burns, R., Curtmola, R., Herring, J., Kissner, L., Peterson, Z., et al.: Provable data possession at untrusted stores. In: Proceedings of the 14th ACM Conference on Computer and Communications Security. Alexandria, Virginia, USA, pp. 598–609 ACM (2007)
17. Juels, A., Kaliski, B.S.: VIP: PORs: Proofs of Retrievability for Large Files, pp. 584–97 (2007)
18. Bellare, M., Goldreich, O.: On defining proofs of knowledge. In: Brickell, E.F. (ed.) CRYPTO 1992. LNCS, vol. 740, pp. 390–420. Springer, Heidelberg (1993). https://doi.org/10.1007/3-540-48071-4_28
19. Shacham, H., Waters, B.: Compact proofs of retrievability. J. Cryptol. **26**(3), 442–483 (2012). https://doi.org/10.1007/s00145-012-9129-2
20. Boneh, D., Lynn, B., Shacham, H.: Short signatures from the Weil pairing. J. Cryptol. **17**(4), 297–319 (2004)
21. Wang, Q., Wang, C., Li, J., Ren, K., Lou, W.: Enabling public verifiability and data dynamics for storage security in cloud computing. In: Backes, M., Ning, P. (eds.) ESORICS 2009. LNCS, vol. 5789, pp. 355–370. Springer, Heidelberg (2009). https://doi.org/10.1007/978-3-642-04444-1_22
22. Wang, B., Li, B., Li, H.: Oruta: privacy-preserving public auditing for shared data in the cloud. IEEE Trans. Cloud Comput. **2**(1), 43–56 (2014)
23. Zhang, X., Xu, C., Zhang, X.: Efficient pairing-free privacy-preserving auditing scheme for cloud storage in distributed sensor networks. Int. J. Distrib. Sens. Netw. **11**(7), 593759 (2015)
24. Shen, J., Shen, J., Chen, X., Huang, X., Susilo, W.: An efficient public auditing protocol with novel dynamic structure for cloud data-pairing based. IEEE Trans. Inf. Forensics Secur. **12**(10), 2402–2415 (2017). https://doi.org/10.1109/tifs.2017.2705620
25. Wang, J., Peng, F., Tian, H., Chen, W., Lu, J.: Public auditing of log integrity for cloud storage systems via blockchain. In: Li, J., Liu, Z., Peng, H. (eds.) SPNCE 2019. LNICSSITE, vol. 284, pp. 378–387. Springer, Cham (2019). https://doi.org/10.1007/978-3-030-21373-2_29

26. Han, J., Li, Y., Chen, W.: VIP$_a lightweight and privacy-preserving public cloud auditing scheme without bilinear pairings in smart cities. Comput. Stand. Interfaces 62, 84–97 (2019). https://doi.org/10.1016/j.csi.2018.08.004

27. Shao, B., Ji, Y.: Efficient TPA-based auditing scheme for secure cloud storage. Clust. Comput. 24(3), 1989–2000 (2021). https://doi.org/10.1007/s10586-021-03239-x

28. Chen, D., Yuan, H., Hu, S., Wang, Q., Wang, C.: BOSSA: a decentralized system for proofs of data retrievability and replication. IEEE Trans. Parallel Distrib. Syst. 32(4), 786–798 (2020)

29. ALmarwani, R., Zhang, N., Garside, J.: An effective, secure and efficient tagging method for integrity protection of outsourced data in a public cloud storage. Plos one 15(11), e0241236 (2020)

30. Li, C., Wang, P., Sun, C., Zhou, K., Huang, P.: $WiBPA: an efficient data integrity auditing scheme without bilinear pairings. Comput. Mater. Continua. 58(2), 319–333 (2019)

31. Liu, C., Chen, J., Yang, L.T., Zhang, X., Yang, C., Ranjan, R., et al.: Authorized public auditing of dynamic big data storage on cloud with efficient verifiable fine-grained updates. IEEE Trans. Parallel Distrib. Syst. 25(9), 2234–2244 (2014). https://doi.org/10.1109/tpds.201 3.191

32. Cash, D., Küpçü, A., Wichs, D.: Dynamic proofs of retrievability via oblivious RAM. J. Cryptol. 30(1), 22–57 (2015). https://doi.org/10.1007/s00145-015-9216-2

33. Ren, Z., Wang, L., Wang, Q., Xu, M.: Dynamic proofs of retrievability for coded cloud storage systems. IEEE Trans. Serv. Comput. 11(4), 685–698 (2018). https://doi.org/10.1109/tsc.2015. 2481880

34. Erway, C.C., Küpçü, A., Papamanthou, C., Tamassia, R.: Dynamic provable data possession. ACM Trans. Inf. Syst. Secur. (TISSEC). 17(4), 15 (2015)

35. Wang, C., Wang, Q., Ren, K., Cao, N., Lou, W.: Toward secure and dependable storage services in cloud computing. IEEE Trans. Serv. Comput. 5(2), 220-232 (2012)

36. Merkle, R.C.: A certified digital signature. In: Brassard, G. (ed.) CRYPTO 1989. LNCS, vol. 435, pp. 218–238. Springer, New York (1990). https://doi.org/10.1007/0-387-34805-0_21

37. Pugh, W.: Skip lists: a probabilistic alternative to balanced trees. Commun. ACM 33(6), 668–676 (1990)

38. Goldreich, O., Ostrovsky, R.: Software protection and simulation on oblivious RAMs. J. ACM (JACM). 43(3), 431–473 (1996)

39. Ateniese, G., Pietro, R., Mancini, L., Gene, T.: Scalable and efficient provable data possession. In: Proceedings of the 4th International Conference on Security and Privacy in Communication Networks (2008)

40. Gan, Q., Wang, X., Fang, X.: VIP22/6_Efficient and secure auditing scheme for outsourced big data with dynamicity in cloud- Algebraic signature. Sci. Chin. Inf. Sci. 61(12), 1–15 (2018)

41. Tian, H., Chen, Y., Chang, C.-C., Jiang, H., Huang, Y., Chen, Y., et al.: Dynamic-hash-table based public auditing for secure cloud storage. IEEE Trans. Serv. Comput. 10(5), 701–714 (2015)

42. Jin, H., Jiang, H., Zhou, K.: Dynamic and public auditing with fair arbitration for cloud data. IEEE Trans. Cloud Comput. 6(3), 680–693 (2018). https://doi.org/10.1109/TCC.2016.252 5998

43. Erway, C.C.: Dynamic provable data possession_important. In: Proceedings of the 16th ACM Conference on Computer and Communications Security, Ccs 2009 (2009)

44. Ateniese, G., Burns, R., Curtmola, R., Herring, J., Khan, O., Kissner, L., et al.: Remote data checking using provable data possession. ACM Trans. Inf. Syst. Secur. 14(1), 1–34 (2011)

45. Zhen, M., Yian, Z., Shigang, C.: A dynamic Proof of Retrievability (PoR) scheme with O(logn) complexity. In: 2012 IEEE International Conference on Communications (ICC), pp. 912–916 (2012)

46. Shi, E., Stefanov, E., Papamanthou, C.: Practical dynamic proofs of retrievability. In: Proceedings of the 2013 ACM SIGSAC Conference on Computer & Communications Security, pp. 325–336. ACM (2013)

47. Chen, J., Peng, Y., Du, R., Yuan, Q., Zheng, M.: Regenerating-codes-based efficient remote data checking and repairing in cloud storage. In: Proceedings - 14th IEEE International Conference on Trust, Security and Privacy in Computing and Communications, pp. 143–150. TrustCom (2015)

48. Sengupta, B., Ruj, S.: Efficient proofs of retrievability with public verifiability for dynamic cloud storage. IEEE Trans. Cloud Comput. 8(1), 138–151 (2020). https://doi.org/10.1109/tcc.2017.2767584

49. Razaque, A., Rizvi, S.S.: Privacy preserving model: a new scheme for auditing cloud stakeholders. J. Cloud Comput. 6(1), 1–17 (2017). https://doi.org/10.1186/s13677-017-0076-1

50. Zheng, Q., Xu, S.: Fair and dynamic proofs of retrievability. In: Proceedings of the First ACM Conference on Data and Application Security and Privacy, San Antonio, TX, USA, pp. 237–48. ACM (2011)

51. Wang, Q., Cong, W., Ren, K., Lou, W., Jin, L.: Enabling public auditability and data dynamics for storage security in cloud computing. IEEE Trans.Parallel and Distrib. Syst. 22(5), 847–859 (2011)

52. Li, J., Tan, X., Chen, X., Wong, D.S., Xhafa, F.: OPoR: Enabling Proof of Retrievability in Cloud Computing with Resource-Constrained Devices. IEEE Trans. Cloud Comput. 2(3), 195–205 (2015)

53. Fu, A., Li, Y., Yu, S., Yu, Y., Zhang, G.: DIPOR: an IDA-based dynamic proof of retrievability scheme for cloud storage systems. J. Netw. Comput. Appl. 104, 97–106 (2018)

54. Zhu, Y., Ahn, G.J., Hu, H., Yau, S.S., An, H.G., Hu, C.J.: Dynamic audit services for outsourced storages in clouds. IEEE Trans. Serv. Comput. 6(2), 227–238 (2013). https://doi.org/10.1109/TSC.2011.51

AI, Expert Systems and Big Data Analytics

A Review of Optical Character Recognition (OCR) Techniques on Bengali Scripts

Md. Imdadul Haque Emon$^{(\boxtimes)}$, Khondoker Nazia Iqbal,
Md Humaion Kabir Mehedi, Mohammed Julfikar Ali Mahbub,
and Annajiat Alim Rasel

Department of Computer Science and Engineering, Brac University, 66 Mohakhali,
Dhaka 1212, Bangladesh
{md.imdadul.haque.emon,khondoker.nazia.iqbal,humaion.kabir.mehedi,
mohammed.julfikar.ali.mahbub}@g.bracu.ac.bd, annajiat@bracu.ac.bd

Abstract. The technique of transforming analogue documents into digital documents using document images is known as Optical Character Recognition (OCR). Since the mid-1980s, researchers have been studying Bangla character recognition. OCR works for Bengali scripts have received a lot of attention but only few works have been done in this field because of the less availability of Bangla resources. Our paper provides an overview of different OCR techniques for Bengali characters. We studied through a total of 13 papers and prepared a summary about previously applied OCR techniques in Bengali language. We also discussed the methodologies used in different steps of OCR. We analyzed performances of those applied techniques on different datasets. From the review papers, the most promising performance was seen using a BLSTM network which achieved 99.32% accuracy in Bengali character recognition.

Keywords: Optical Character Recognition (OCR) · Bengali scripts · Digital documents

1 Introduction

The process of transforming handwritten and scanned text documents into digital documents is known as OCR. In this technique, each character on a page is scanned individually. Optical Character Recognition started as a branch of pattern recognition, deep learning, and vision based research. An Austrian engineer named "Gustav Tauschek" developed the first OCR machine in the late 1920s [1].

The most important technique for automatic text identification till date is optical character recognition (OCR). It has significantly enhanced the data entering procedure. We may make mistakes while copying data from an image to the computer. However, utilizing OCR technology, we can accurately transcribe picture documents into text documents. OCR also helps to save time and money

M. H. Miraz et al. (Eds.): iCETiC 2022, LNICST 463, pp. 85–94, 2023.
https://doi.org/10.1007/978-3-031-25161-0_6

by eliminating the need to manually enter data from scanned documents into a computer. In addition, we are unable to look for and change important information included in electronic images and pdf documents. OCR can help solve this problem by converting digital images and pdf files into modifiable and searchable digital text documents.

OCR technology has been used in several established languages throughout the world for many years. However, because Bangla is a low-resource language, OCR research in Bangla began in the late 1980s [2]. Bangla characters are more complex in form than other languages such as English, Arabic, French, etc. In addition, there are approximately 334 complex characters in the Bangla language. These characters are made up of many different of Bengali characters [3]. As a result, developing an OCR for Bangla is more complex than for other languages. For this reason, we have summarised previously implemented OCR technology for the Bangla language in our study, which will be useful for future research in this field.

In Sect. 2 of this paper, we have summarized previously published work in this field. We gave an overview of the basic properties of Bengali scripts in Sect. 3. Section 4 contains information on the datasets utilized in various research work. Recognition techniques and preprocessing stages then are outlined in Sect. 5. Next, Sect. 6 includes the result part. Finally, Sect. 6 brings our paper to a conclusion.

2   Related Works

Till date, multiple approaches have been applied by researchers for optical character recognition in the Bangla language. In this work, we have analyzed a total of 13 relevant research papers for OCR in Bangla.

In 2008, Hasnat et al. have presented an OCR system for detecting Bangla characters using the Hidden Markov Model in his research article [4]. An open source Tesseract engine [5] by Hasnat et al. was utilized for identifying Bangla scripts in another research in 2009. Farisa et al. also constructed an OCR design employing different CNN architectures such as DenseNet, NasNet, and MobileNet in their research article [6] which was published in 2021. To improve Bangla OCR output, in 2016 some researchers used N-gram and Edit distance algorithms [7]. Neural networks are used as a better approach for detection of Bangla characters in a research in 2002 [8]. Another research by Adnan et al. [9] which was conducted in 2007, used a Kohonen neural network to classify Bangla characters in the OCR system. In 2012, back propagation neural network approach is used in a work by Ahmed et al. [10] to recognize printed Bangla scripts. Paul et al. [11] used a single hidden BLSTM framework for printed Bengali OCR systems in 2019.

The summary of our reviewed papers are listed in the below Table 1.

Table 1. Related works in OCR for Bengali scripts

Paper	Technique	Dataset
Hasnat et al. [4]	HMM	Alphabets of Bangla Character set
Hasnat et al. [5]	Tesseract	All the characters of Bangla language
Farisa et al. [6]	DenseNet, NasNet, MobileNet	Bengali Writing Dataset [12]
Sajib et al. [7]	N-gram and Edit Distance	83,570 words from different Online portals
Ahmed et al. [8]	Neural Network	Characters of Sutonny, Sulekha and Modhumati font
Adnan et al. [9]	Kohonen Network	Single characters and single word images
Shamim et al. [10]	Back Propagation Neural Network	Hundred thousand words from Bangla books, papers, and sixty thousand words from Bangla dictionary
Paul et al. [11]	The BLSTM-CTC architecture	47,720 Text line images
Mahbub et al. [13]	Multilayer Feed Neural Network	Sutonny, Sulekha, Sunetra Fonts
Pal et al. [14]	A Feature based Tree classifier	Text documents from manually composed books containing 5000 characters in each

3 Properties of Bengali Scripts

Bangla language has the most complex-shaped characters than other languages. Bengali script is generally divided into two classes: vowels and consonants. There are 50 characters in all, including 11 vowels and 49 consonants[1]. There are also various modifiers and compound characters in Bengali scripts. Two or more consonants are combined to make compound characters. As the English characters, Bangla characters doesn't have any upper or lower case letters. But there is a new term in Bangla known as 'Matra' which is basically a horizontal line above the letters. Some characters are with 'Matra' and some characters have no 'Matra'. All these characteristics of Bangla alphabets are making very difficult to implement the OCR for Bangla. Some examples of Bangla alphabets are shown below in Table 2.

---

[1] https://en.wikipedia.org/wiki/Bengali_alphabet.

Table 2. Example of Bangla characters

Vowels	অ, আ, ই, ঈ, উ, ঊ, ঋ, এ, ঐ, ও, ঔ
Consonants	ক, খ, গ, ঘ, ঙ, চ, ছ, জ, ঝ, ঞ, ট, ঠ, ড, ঢ, ণ, ত, থ, দ, ধ, ন, প, ফ, ব, ভ, ম, য, র, ল, হ, শ, ষ, স, য়, ড়, ঢ়, ৎ, ০৫, ০৪, ঁ
Vowel Modifiers	া, ি, ী, ু, ৄ, ৃ, ে, ৈ, ো, ৌ
Compound Letters	ক্ব, জ্ঞ, ত্র, ম্ন, ম্ম, ধ্ব, ক্ষ, ক্র

4   Dataset

Handwritten characters and machine printed images are two forms of OCR data for the Bangla language. Since Bangla is a low-resource language, the dataset is insufficient. Farisa et al. [6] in their paper used the Bangla Handwriting Dataset [12], which comprises 21,234 words gathered from the handwriting of 260 people. Some examples of the handwritten image data are shown in below Fig. 1 and Fig. 2. To train their model, some researchers utilized various Bangla font characters such as Sutonny, Sulekha, Modhumati, and Sunetra. Furthermore, Shamim et al. [10] have gathered hundred thousand words from Bangla publications and newspapers, as well as roughly sixty thousand words from the Bangla dictionary, for their research. The list of the datasets used in our reviewed papers are shown in the Table 1.

5   Recognition Techniques

Different models were used in our reviewed publications to recognize Bangla characters in handwritten texts and scanned documents. CNN models (DenseNet121, NesNet, MobileNet), neural network models (Multilayer feed forward network, Back Propagation neural network, Kohonen Network), HMM, BLSTM, N-gram, and Edit Distance are some of the commonly used models in this domain.

Although numerous approaches can be used to develop OCR technology, there are several basic processes that are followed in all 11 papers. The steps are as follows:

1. Preprocessing
2. Feature Extraction
3. Pattern Recognition and Classification
4. Post Processing

5.1 Preprocessing

Some basic steps of preprocessing are described below:

- **Text Digitization and Binarization:**
  The popular techniques used in text digitization are Flat-bed scanner and
  hand-held scanner. Most of our reviewed papers, [4, 7, 13, 14] used Flat-bed
  scanner for digitization purpose. The technique of transforming gray scale
  photos to binary photos is known as Binarization. There are different Binarization techniques: Niblack's Algorithm, Otsu Global Algorithm, Global
  Fixed Threshold [15], etc. In some of our reviewed papers, Otsu Global algorithm is used and most of them used threshold approach for image Binarization.

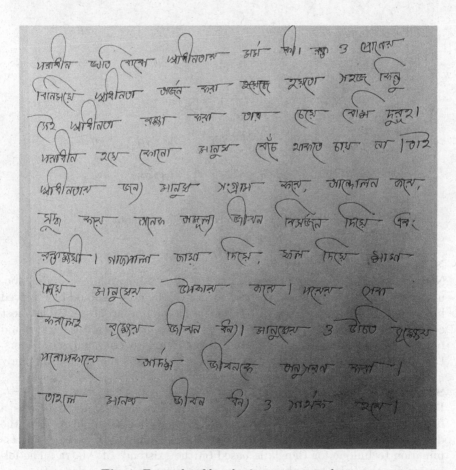

Fig. 1. Example of handwritten raw text data

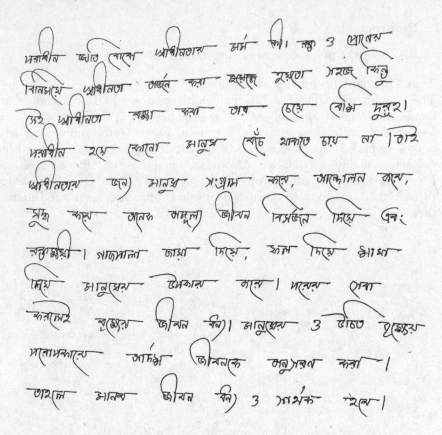

Fig. 2. Example of handwritten binary data

– **Noise Removal:**
Noise removal is an essential step of data preprocessing. While scanning documents or images, it can be corrupted by noise. The noises should be removed before data processing to recognize Bangla characters accurately. The most common noises for the printed and scanned documents are the background noises and the salt and pepper noises. According to our analysed papers, Low-pass filters, wiener filters and median filters are the most commonly used techniques for noise removal.

– **Skew Detection and Correction:**
Papers can be skewed during scanning with different scanners, such as a hand-held scanner or a flat-bed scanner, therefore it is required to align the documents accurately before sending them for training. The skewness determination technique for Bangla is based on the existence of 'Matra'. The following are the basic two phases in removing skewness from a dataset:

1. Calculate the value of skew angle Θt
2. Image rotation in the opposite direction of the skew angle Θt

– **Segmentation:**
Various forms of segmentation are carried out during preprocessing. Lines, words, and characters can all be segmented. Greedy search technique and Contour tracing techniques are used in the character segmentation process (Fig. 3).

Fig. 3. Word segmentation from printed documents [16]

5.2   Feature Extraction

We need to extract the features after the preprocessing. Each character must be represented as a vector in order to extract the features. To extract features, Mahbub et al. [13] applied scaled character and the Freeman chain code in their research. Hasnat et al. [4], on the other hand, separated the preprocessed images into distinct frames of a predetermined length. Then they calculated Discrete Cosine Transform for each pixel in the frames. To extract features from images, some publications applied the DFS approach, while others used the RNN model. In their study, Shamim et al. [10] focused on distinguishing connected components in a character in order to extract properties from the input images. They extracted connected components from each character using the DFS method. In their research, Farisa et al. [6] introduced two processes for extracting features from an input image. Initially, a baseline model is utilized, which accepts images as input and produces high-dimensional characteristics as output. CNN based models: DenseNet, NasNet, MobileNet are used to build their baseline model. The output of the baseline model is then supplied as input to a bidirectional RNN model in the second stage. To tackle the gradient problem of the RNN model, they applied LSTM and Gated Recurrent Unit (GRU). Finally, the output of the RNN model is used by additional models for pattern recognition.

5.3   Pattern Recognition and Classification

The key aspect of OCR for Bangla is pattern recognition and categorization. All extracted characteristics are compared to the training dataset in this stage to identify and categorize Bangla characters. In a paper [13], a multi-layer feed forward is utilized to detect and categorize Bangla letter patterns. A temporary model and a Hidden Markov Model Toolkit (HTK) recognizer are used to discover patterns in another work [4]. Back propagation recognizer, a common multi-layer network learning approach, has been applied in the research work of

[10] to solve pattern categorization problems. Tesseract was utilized in Hasnat et al. [5] paper to identify patterns and produce text data from OCR. To categorize Bangla characters, a paper [11] for the printed Bengali OCR system, used 166 class labels. Adnan et al. [6] utilized the Kohonen network to identify patterns. In a study [14], a template machine approach is developed for categorization problems. Furthermore, To identify and recognize Bangla characters, Ahmed et al. [8] utilized a Neural network.

5.4 Post Processing

The OCR system's final phase is post-processing. This stage is carried out once the texts have been identified and categorised. The recognized texts don't always match the source texts. Various post-processing stages, including as error checking, spell checking, and text editing, are used to remedy these mistakes. In their study, Hasnat et al. [4] developed a suggestion-based spell checker to fix textual mistakes. Rather than replacing words with inaccuracies, they use a different technique to suggest other ways to correct those words. In the post processing step, edit distance technique along with N-gram algorithms are used by the authors of a work on improving Bangla OCR output [7].

6 Result Analysis

The articles we looked at used a variety of techniques to implement a Bengali OCR system. In the Multilayer Feed Forward Network approach [13], authors trained their neural network with the feature vector which was generated for every character in their training set and these characters were detected from the prior knowledge of their neural network. Hasnat et al. achieved around 98% accuracy using Hidden Markov Model (HMM) [4] and they used an error correcting module which fixes the splitting error of characters due to not having "full matra". Ahmed et al. used a "Back Propagation Neural Network" [10] to compare the output vector with the targetted vector and this method recognises optical character with 97.5% accuracy with completely unseen samples. On another research by Hasnat et al., recognition was performed using the Tesseract engine [5] which showed about 93% accuracy on average. A neural network [8] with input vector dimention of 256, output dimention of 60 and 40 hidden layer performed 96.33% accuracy while using a font size of 12. A research by Shatil [9] used a Kohonen Network with no hidden layer can recognise optical character with 99% accuracy for scanned documents. A feature based Tree Classifier by Pal et al. [14] scored 96.55%. And at last, research by Paul and CHaudhuri [11] showed that a single hidden BLSTM-CTC method can perform a wooping 99.32% at optical character recognition.

The character level accuracy rate and error rate are displayed in Table 3 and Table 4.

Table 3. Accuracy score

Model	Accuracy
Multilayer feed forward network	97%
HMM	98%
Back Propagation	97.5%
Tesseract	93%
Neural Network	96.33%
Kohonen Network	99%
Tree Classifier	96.55%
BLSTM-CTC	99.32%

Table 4. Error rate

Model	Error rate
DenseNet121+GRU	0.091
Edit Distance	0.1685
N-gram approach	0.1716

We can conclude from the accuracy level that BLSTM-CTC architecture obtained the highest accuracy when it comes to developing OCR for the Bangla language.

7   Conclusion

In this paper we reported various works on OCR for Bengali scripts. We looked at a total of 13 papers, 10 of which applied different approaches to develop an OCR and 3 of them provided an overview of Bangla OCR. We discovered through our research that several types of Neural Networks are commonly utilized in Bengali character identification and categorization. Furthermore, the BLSTM network achieved the highest accuracy in Bengali character recognition, with 99.32% accuracy, according to our research. Our survey will encourage researchers to work on Bangla OCR. It will help researchers to build an OCR for Bangla, which will be able to detect and classify Bengali characters from both handwritten and scanned documents.

References

1. Optical character recognition - history of optical character recognition (OCR) (2021). https://history-computer.com/opticalcharacter-recognition-history-of-optical-character-recognition-ocr/. Accessed 12 Dec 2021

2. Ahmed, T., Raihan, M.N., Kushol, R., Salekin, M.S.: A complete Bangla optical character recognition system: an effective approach. In: 2019 22nd International Conference on Computer and Information Technology (ICCIT), pp. 1–7 (2019). https://doi.org/10.1109/ICCIT48885.2019.9038551
3. Das, N., Acharya, K., Sarkar, R., Basu, S., Kundu, M., Nasipuri, M.: A benchmark image database of isolated Bangla handwritten compound characters. Int. J. Doc. Anal. Recogn. (IJDAR) **17**, 413–431 (2014). https://doi.org/10.1007/s10032-014-0222-y
4. Hasnat, M.A., Habib, S.M., Khan, M.: A high performance domain specific OCR for Bangla script. In: Sobh, T., Elleithy, K., Mahmood, A., Karim, M.A. (eds.) Novel Algorithms and Techniques in Telecommunications, Automation and Industrial Electronics, pp. 174–178. Springer, Cham (2008). https://doi.org/10.1007/978-1-4020-8737-0_31
5. Hasnat, M.A., Chowdhury, M.R., Khan, M.: An open source tesseract based optical character recognizer for Bangla script. In: 2009 10th International Conference on Document Analysis and Recognition, pp. 671–675. IEEE (2009)
6. Safir, F.B., Ohi, A.Q., Mridha, M.F., Monowar, M.M., Hamid, M.A.: End-to-end optical character recognition for Bengali handwritten words. In: 2021 National Computing Colleges Conference (NCCC), pp. 1–7. IEEE (2021)
7. Ahmed, M.S., Gonçalves, T., Sarwar, H.: Improving Bangla OCR output through correction algorithms. In: 2016 10th International Conference on Software, Knowledge, Information Management & Applications (SKIMA), pp. 338–343. IEEE (2016)
8. Chowdhury, A.A., Ahmed, E., Ahmed, S., Hossain, S., Rahman, C.M.: Optical character recognition of Bangla characters using neural network: a better approach. In: 2nd ICEE. Citeseer (2002)
9. Shatil, A.M., et al.: Research report on Bangla optical character recognition using Kohonen network. Technical report, BRAC University (2007)
10. Ahmed, S., Sakib, A.N., Ishtiaque Mahmud, M., Belali, H., Rahman, S.: The anatomy of Bangla OCR system for printed texts using back propagation neural network. Glob. J. Comput. Sci. Technol. (2012)
11. Paul, D., Chaudhuri, B.B.: A BLSTM network for printed Bengali OCR system with high accuracy. arXiv preprint arXiv:1908.08674 (2019)
12. Biswas, M., Islam, R., Shom, G.K., et al.: Banglalekha-isolated: a multipurpose comprehensive dataset of handwritten Bangla isolated characters. Data Brief **12**, 103–107 (2017)
13. Alam, M.M., Kashem, M.A.: A complete Bangla OCR system for printed characters. JCIT **1**(01), 30–35 (2010)
14. Pal, U., Chaudhuri, B.: OCR in Bangla: an Indo-Bangladeshi language. In: Proceedings of the 12th IAPR International Conference on Pattern Recognition, vol. 3-Conference C: Signal Processing (Cat. No. 94CH3440-5), vol. 2, pp. 269–273. IEEE (1994)
15. Kibria, M.G., Al-Imtiaz: Bengali optical character recognition using self organizing map. In: 2012 International Conference on Informatics, Electronics Vision (ICIEV), pp. 764–769 (2012). https://doi.org/10.1109/ICIEV2012.6317479
16. Omee, F.Y., Himel, S.S., Bikas, M.A.N.: A complete workflow for development of Bangla OCR. arXiv preprint arXiv:1204.1198 (2012)

Traffic Sign Detection and Recognition System Using Improved YOLOV5s

Md. Ariful Hossain[✉], Anwar Hossain, and Md. Ismail Jabiullah

Daffodil International University, Dhaka, Bangladesh
{ariful15-12473,anwar15-12699,drismail.cse}@diu.edu.bd

Abstract. Traffic sign detection is one of the most challenging tasks for autonomous vehicles, especially for the detection of different types of signs and real-time applications. Unmanned driving systems face a lot of problems to recognize traffic signs faster and more accurately. In this paper, we propose a model using improved YOLOv5 to detect Traffic signs and recognize them properly. Our dataset consists of 3500 pictures of the traffic sign and we have annotated all that pictures in YOLOv5 format. There is 39 classification of our dataset on all pictures based on the traffic sign. This system can be used for unmanned driving vehicles. Using this model a device can make which will help drivers who are driving a car. After implementation of our dataset with the help of improved YOLOv5, the output shows an accuracy of 86.75% in different conditions such as low light, cloudy, rainy, and sunny.

Keywords: Traffic sign · Autonomous vehicle · Unmanned driving · YOLOv5 · Annotation

1 Introduction

Object detection has taken one of the most important places in this modern era. That's why it took the attention of researchers in real-world application and academic study purposes in the field of deep learning, neural network, and computer vision. For example, autonomous driving, human detection, ensuring security, and robot vision. Among all of them, autonomous driving is getting more important day by day cause it provides accurate service in time with reducing human effort. Here autonomous vehicles [1] use the process of Traffic sign detection. Many renowned companies of this world are willing to invest in the autonomous system for their car for their worldwide demand. Such as Tesla, Cruise, Mercedes-Benz, BMW, Uber, Ford, Honda, and Hyundai. Deep learning [2] helps in traffic sign detection is a timely response, perfect maintenance, making decisions overall getting a smart service. In previous times traffic sign detection had been done manually by using machine learning. Where the pictures of traffic signs were captured by a camera which was connected by cars. To recognize those pictures a human used to detect traffic signs manually by comparing existing databases. But today we do not need to use this manually cause there has been some updated process

© ICST Institute for Computer Sciences, Social Informatics and Telecommunications Engineering 2023
Published by Springer Nature Switzerland AG 2023. All Rights Reserved
M. H. Miraz et al. (Eds.): iCETiC 2022, LNICST 463, pp. 95–106, 2023.
https://doi.org/10.1007/978-3-031-25161-0_7

by using smart way with computer vision. Object detection is two types. Two-stage detector and One-stage detector [3]. Two-stage detector use object region proposal and object classification. Some detectors are Region-based Convolutional Neural Network (R-CNN) [4], Fast Region-based Convolutional Neural Network (Fast R-CNN) [5], Faster Region-based Convolutional Neural Network (Faster R-CNN) [6], and Mask Region-based Convolutional Neural Network (Mask R-CNN) [7]. One stage detector involves the bounding boxes predicted over the images without the region proposal. Some detectors are You Only Look Once (Yolo) [8], yolov2, yolov3, yolov4, yolov5, and M2Det [9]. From all of them, Yolov5 is the most famous one for this platform cause of its accurate result and perfect detection system. It is also good for real-time object detection. In this paper, we use Yolov5 to detect traffic signs.

2   Literature Review

Now this time the world working with digital videos and images. Artificial Intelligence is one of the most common topics to do this job for moderate any sector or getting any kind of recognition on a particular matter. Specifically, computer vision works for image or video processing in Artificial Intelligence. In deep learning, the YoloV5 [10] algorithm comes to detect objects accurately.

Already there had done a lot of research work in this segment with Yolo V5. Researchers work on different subjects for the various topic. They had taken several types of datasets for done their job or make something new such as maritime, traffic signs, human, animal, food, disease, etc. In our paper, we are working on a traffic sign detection and recognition system [11] to contribute in autonomous vehicle fields. In some papers, they work for traffic sign detection for any particular country rules for example, German Traffic Sign Benchmark (GTSB) [12], Sweden Traffic Sign(STS) [13], Belgium Traffic Sign(BTS) [14], The Netherland Traffic Sign(NTS) [14], France Traffic Sign(FTS), The United States Traffic Sign(UTS) [14] and Iraqi Traffic Sign Detection Benchmark(IQTSDB) [15]. But in this paper, we are contributing to building a model which can be used in the entire world to detect traffic signs.

Thus, this model will recognize any kind of traffic sign in a global way. A traffic sign can be national or international, that's why we should not bound in any limited area to recognize them. Here our model working on this topic to find any kind of traffic sign nationally or internationally. Apparently this model will be helpful all over the world in different issues. Many country have similar traffic sign such as speed sign at all range, stop and traffic light color. So, we have focused on those sign to merge traffic sign to bulid a robust model.

Till now all researchers doing their jobs on traffic sign detection only, they did not focus on autonomous driving strategy. Here we are covering both sides in our paper. We have a class named 'Car' in our dataset which helps us to build the model and this model can detect cars from the real-time dataset.

3 Methodology

3.1 Dataset

In our proposed model we have used a dataset of the traffic sign. We collect our data from different sources on the internet. All these images have been captured by the camera installed in vehicles and mobile cameras. These pictures are taken depending on various environments, conditions, and time duration. Here we used 39 classes of data for our dataset. There have 3324 high-resolution images. We used 2315 images for training, 685 images for validation, and 324 images for testing. Usually, traffic signs are divided into 4 categories such Mandatory, Warning, Prohibitory, and Directory.

Table 1. Thirty nine class of traffic signs divided into four catogories.

Category	Classes
Mandatory signs	Turn Left, Turn Right, End of Right Road -Go straight, Go Left or Straight, Go Right or Straight, Go Straight
Warning signs	Danger Ahead, Left Curve Ahead, Left Sharp Curve, Huddle Road, Traffic Signals Ahead, Snow Warning Sign, Slippery Road, Right Sharp Curve, Road Work, Right Curve Ahead, Cycle Zone, Deer Zone
Prohibitory signs	No Entry, No Over Taking Trucks, No Over Taking, No Stopping, No Waiting, Speed Limit 100, Speed Limit 120, Speed Limit 30, Speed Limit 50, Speed Limit 60, Speed Limit 70, Speed Limit 80, Stop, human, Car
Directory signs	Give Way, Green Signal, Pedestrian, Red Signal, Truck Sign, Yellow Signal

Moreover, we used the image augmentation technique here. That's why our dataset volume extends more than before.

3.2 Image Annotation

To make a model for detecting objects from images or video firstly it is important to annotate images. By annotating images model can classify and recognize the object precisely and more accurately. We also annotate our images to run our model properly. Here we used LabelImg Software to annotate all traffic sign images. Using this software we had done two parts of the job to annotate images, they are class labeling and bounding box. We had done these two jobs manually. At the time of image annotation, we create a rectangular box around the traffic sign. While it faces multiple object images we label them individually. After labeling all the bounding boxes the file save in XML format at that we convert this file into YoloV5 PyTorch txt format.

3.3 Architecture

Yolo v5 follows a structural way to build any model on any kind of dataset. Yolo v5 is known as a single-stage object detector. In Yolo v5 architecture there have three important parts such as:

1. Backbone stage
2. Neck (PANet) stage
3. Head stage

We maintain this three-stage to run our model. Yolo v5 algorithm performs better in (416 * 416) dimensional images. Usually, images are set in different dimensions. Firstly we have resized the images from our collected dataset. Then resized images passed through the three stages of Yolo v5.

Backbone Stage: After passing our images as input in the backbone stage extract all important features from the given pictures of our dataset. At first, our given images go through the focus layer of the backbone stage. This layer decreases resolution and increases the depths of images. Then the output overpass from Convolutional and BottleNeckCSP layers [16]. In the meantime, feature extracts individually here for different pictures. At the end of this stage the output will go via the SPP layer. This layer is also called the pooling layer.

Neck Stage (PANet): The output of BottleNeckCSP goes through SPP (Spiral Pyramid Pooling) block to expand the receptive field and then distinguish the important features. This SPP is comparatively better than other CNN (Convolutional Neural Network) based model layers cause it can process input images of any dimension. Ultimately the goal of the SPP layer is to generate an output of fixed dimension. SPP layer distinguishes important features by making its multi-scale version. This SPP layer can make N number of multi-scale versions. These same features can be separated simultaneously in N number of blocks.

PANet [17] stage stands for Path Aggregation Network. Here the sequence of network layers is responsible to mix and aggregate the features of images. PAN is an updated version of Feature Pyramid Network (FPN). The backbone contains a lot of layers because of the presence of the deep neural network. Previously, on FPN it had to go through a long path to flow features from low-level to high-level layers. But In PAN there have a shortcut to connect fine-grained features from the top and bottom layers. Concatenation layers help combine the layers and give a shortcut for better and quicker performance.

Head Stage: This stage is situated to detect the last step in this process. The Head stage is mainly used to perform the final detection part. In this step, we apply anchor boxes to our processed data to resize them precisely. Then finally it generates the output with different classes such as objectiveness scores, probabilities, and bounding boxes as we had done the grid sells at the first steps but here are the final bounding boxes to recognize clearly and finally. The main structure of this architecture is shown in Fig. 1.

Overview of YOLOv5

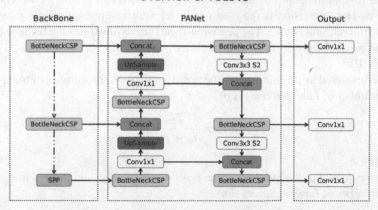

Fig. 1. The structure of the stage architecture.

Before digging deep into object detection with the important metrics of evaluation, some basic concepts need to be clear. Whenever we start talking about object detection, several definitions that are useful listing in below:

Intersection over Union (IoU):

In IoU, firstly evaluates the intersection area from the two bounding boxes, the ground truth bounding box, and the predicted bounding box. Then divide the intersection area by the union area of those bounding boxes (In figure). Concerning all this, a prediction can be categorized into True Positive or Valid and False Positive or Invalid.

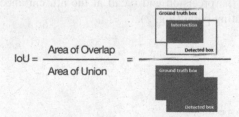

True Positive (TP): It denotes that the detection is correct. The IoU ratio is used to determine whether the prediction is Right or Wrong followed by a given threshold. Typically, the threshold is set at 50%, 75%, 85%, or 95%. Using this threshold we can define the behavior of the outputs. Like, any object detector system can perform better at a 50% threshold but it will not be easy when the threshold is set at 95%.

False Positive (FP): It means the detection is incorrect. Here, the IoU ratio must have to be under the threshold.

True Negative (TN): The object detection model didn't detect anything. The model predicts that there is no object in the picture and it is correct.

False Negative (FN): It denotes the object didn't detect. The object is present in the picture but the model failed to detect that.

At the time of imbalanced classes, we use precision-recall which is a useful measure of success. Here precision is the measure of relevant results and recalls measure the return of true relevant results. The precision-recall curve illustrates the balance between recall and precision for different entrances.

Precision (P):

It is considered as the number of true positives (Tp) on the number of true positives and the number of false positives (Fp).

$$P = \frac{T_p}{T_p + F_p} \tag{1}$$

Recall (R):

It is considered as the number of true positives (Tp) on the number of true positives and the number of false negatives (Fn).

$$R = \frac{T_p}{T_p + F_n} \tag{2}$$

Harmonic mean (F1) of precision and recall [18]:

$$F1 = 2\frac{P \times R}{P + R} \tag{3}$$

Average precision (AP):

It summarizes such a plot as the weighted mean of precisions achieved at each entrance, with the increase in recall from the previous entrance used as the weight:

$$AP = \sum_n (R_n - R_{n-1})P_n \tag{4}$$

Here, Pn and Rn are the precision and recall at the nth entrance. A pair (Rk, Pk) is referred to as an operating point (Fig. 2).

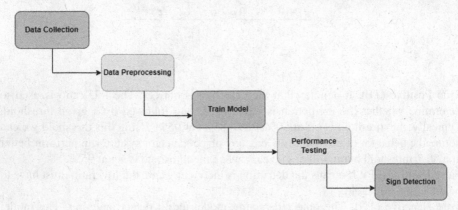

Fig. 2. Workflow of traffic sign model.

At first, we collect the picture of signs from multiple resources. To preprocess all the images we annotated and classify them in different classes. In train model stage, modify the YOLOv5s algorithm to train our model. The following phase test the performance of the traffic sign model using test dataset. Finally, the actual goal of this model is to recognize or detect traffic signs properly.

4 Result and Discussion

In this experiment, we have used Google Colab Pro as our working environment and Python Language with PyTorch for coding. Instead of using the pre-trained COCO weights, we make our custom model by changing the value of the number of classes, data path and to stable the average loss using a momentum value of 0.85. Then started our training using our custom model with 1000 epochs. By using Intel (R) Core(TM) i7-8565U CPU @ 1.80 GHz (CPU) and Intel(R) UHD Graphics 620 (GPU) [19] in windows 10 with Anaconda environment throughout the testing phase. The dataset contains a total of 3324 high-resolution images and used 2315 images for training, 685 images for validation lastly 324 images for testing.

In this research paper, we have used the mean Average Precision (mAP) as the main component to measure the performance of this detection model. The larger percentage or rate of mAP indicates the best accuracy of object detection in the following experiment. Here, the value of mAP can be calculated using the formula given below:

$$mAP = \frac{1}{N} \sum_{i}^{N} AP_i \tag{5}$$

Here, N is the total number of object classes and i denotes the label of a class. Apart from that, in the Precision-Recall Curve (PRC) APi provides the region of that curve, and APi provide the value of Average Precision for each i. These two points 0.5 or 50% and 0.95 or 95% has set as the threshold of IoU to calculate the mAP value. After finishing the final epoch we get the mAP value is 86.75% at IoU 0.5 and 60.1% at IoU 0.95. When the threshold point value IoU is set at 0.5 and 0.95 Fig. 3 represents the best value of mAP in our traffic sign model. Moreover, we have also got a Precision value of 76.2% and a Recall value of 82.9%. Figure 4 shows the curve of Precision and Recall of our training model at final epochs. In opposite, to inspect the prediction of the model and look for any chance to enhance the model performance a confusion matrix has been used with the validation dataset. While training the model validation data was used to evaluate the model performance at each epoch. The Table 1 presents the value of precision equal to 77%, Recall equal to 89%, and F1- Scores equal to 83% at the time of validation at each class. In the experimental result, we see that prohibitory and Directory signs provide the best mAP among all the categories of signs. The Table 2 shows the mAP comparison of all the categories of traffic signs at (IoU = 0.5). At last, the Fig. 5 presents the final predicted result of traffic signs using the model that we have built (Table 3).

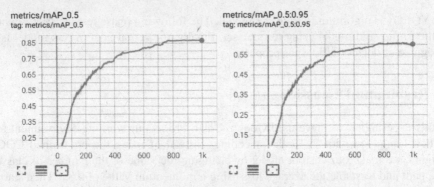

Fig. 3. The greatest value of mAP of the model.

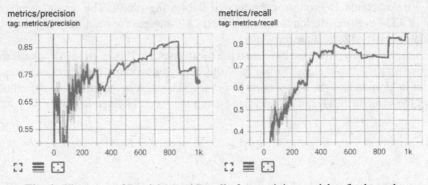

Fig. 4. The curve of Precision and Recall of our training model at final epochs.

Table 2. To present the accuracy rate using the following matrix of each class.

Classes	Scores		
	Precision	Recall	F1-score
Car	0.81	0.96	0.88
Danger Ahead	0.53	0.71	0.61
End of Right Road-Go straight	1.00	1.00	1.00
Give Way	0.85	1.00	0.92
Go Right or Straight	0.92	0.40	0.56
Go Straight	0.63	0.86	0.73
Green Signal	0.72	0.96	0.82
Huddle Road	1.00	0.84	0.91
Left Curve Ahead	1.00	1.00	1.00

(*continued*)

Table 2. (*continued*)

Classes	Scores		
	Precision	Recall	F1-score
Left Sharp Curve	0.49	0.85	0.62
No Entry	0.95	0.91	0.93
No Over Taking Trucks	0.74	0.88	0.80
No Over Taking	0.87	0.86	0.86
No Stopping	0.60	1.00	0.75
No Waiting	0.40	1.00	0.57
Pedestrian	0.98	0.88	0.89
Red Signal	0.69	0.83	0.75
Right Curve Ahead	0.77	0.74	0.75
Right Sharp Curve	0.44	0.69	0.54
Slippery Road	0.79	0.91	0.85
Snow Warning Sign	0.74	1.00	0.85
Speed Limit 100	0.89	0.72	0.80
Speed Limit 120	0.83	0.98	0.90
Speed Limit 30	0.86	0.96	0.91
Speed Limit 50	0.91	1.00	0.95
Speed Limit 60	0.86	0.98	0.92
Speed Limit 70	0.78	0.98	0.89
Speed Limit 80	0.88	0.97	0.92
Stop	0.96	1.00	0.98
Traffic Signals Ahead	0.64	0.83	0.72
Truck Sign	0.89	1.00	0.94
Turn Left	0.12	1.00	0.21
Turn Right	0.56	1.00	0.72
Yellow Signal	1.00	0.66	0.80
human	0.75	0.88	0.81
Total/Avg	0.77	0.89	0.83

Table 3. When IOU = 0.5, comparison of mAP between Categories.

Category	YOLOV5(our model)
Mandatory signs	78%
Warning signs	80%
Prohibitory signs	95%
Directory signs	94%
mAP	86.75%

Fig. 5. The final output of our model.

5 Conclusion

In this paper, we proposed a method of traffic sign detection system based on modified YOLOv5, which provide better performance for recognizing any traffic sign. Here we describe the traffic sign detection and recognition system by focusing on 39 classes for the overall autonomous vehicle concept. We used to gather images from different sources that have been captured in various weather conditions. In this trained model we measured our result depending on mean Average Precision (mAP). Here, the threshold value has been set at IoU = 0.5 and IoU = 0.95 for the model. Our provided model will contribute to the field of autonomous driving systems. In upcoming years, a mobile application can be implemented to detect traffic signs and also using Raspberry Pi a real-time detection and recognition system can be made to help modern society.

References

1. Satilmiş, Y., Tufan, F., Şara, M., Karsli, M., Eken, S., Sayar, A.: CNN based traffic sign recognition for mini autonomous vehicles. In: Świątek, J., Borzemski, L., Wilimowska, Z. (eds.) ISAT 2018. AISC, vol. 853, pp. 85–94. Springer, Cham (2019). https://doi.org/10.1007/978-3-319-99996-8_8
2. Tai, S.K., Dewi, C., Chen, R.C., Liu, Y.T., Jiang, X., Yu, H.: Deep learning for traffic sign recognition based on spatial pyramid pooling with scale analysis. Appl. Sci. **10**(19), 1–16 (2020). https://doi.org/10.3390/app10196997
3. Carranza-García, M., Torres-Mateo, J., Lara-Benítez, P., García-Gutiérrez, J.: On the performance of one-stage and two-stage object detectors in autonomous vehicles using camera data. Remote Sens. **13**(1), 89 (2020). https://doi.org/10.3390/rs13010089
4. Bai, X., Wang, C., Li, C.: A streampath-based RCNN approach to ocean eddy detection. IEEE Access **7**, 106336–106345 (2019). https://doi.org/10.1109/ACCESS.2019.2931781
5. Girshick, R.: Fast R-CNN. In: Proceedings of the IEEE International Conference on Computer Vision, vol. 2015, pp. 1440–1448 (2015). https://doi.org/10.1109/ICCV.2015.169
6. Liu, B., Zhao, W., Sun, Q.: Study of object detection based on faster R-CNN. In: 2017 Chinese Automation Congress (CAC), pp. 6233–6236 (2017). https://doi.org/10.1109/CAC.2017.8243900
7. Sumit, S.S., Watada, J., Roy, A., Rambli, D.R.A.: In object detection deep learning methods, {YOLO} shows supremum to Mask R-{CNN}. In: Journal of Physics: Conference Series, vol. 1529, no. 4, p. 42086 (2020). https://doi.org/10.1088/1742-6596/1529/4/042086
8. Plastiras, G., Kyrkou, C., Theocharides, T.: Efficient convnet-based object detection for unmanned aerial vehicles by selective tile processing. In: ACM International Conference on Proceeding Series (2018). https://doi.org/10.1145/3243394.3243692
9. Zhao, Q., et al.: M2det: a single-shot object detector based on multi-level feature pyramid network. In: 33rd AAAI Conference on Artificial Intelligence, AAAI 2019, 31st Innovation Applications Artificial Intelligence Conference, IAAI 2019, 9th AAAI Symposium Education Advance Artificial Intelligence, EAAI 2019, pp. 9259–9266 (2019). https://doi.org/10.1609/aaai.v33i01.33019259
10. Thuan, D.: Evolution of YOLO Algorithm and YOLOv5: the State-of-the-Art Object Detection Algorithm, p. 61 (2021)
11. Wang, C.: Research and application of traffic sign detection and recognition based on deep learning. In: 2018 International Conference on Robots & Intelligent System (ICRIS), pp. 150–152 (2018). https://doi.org/10.1109/ICRIS.2018.00047

12. Houben, S., Stallkamp, J., Salmen, J., Schlipsing, M., Igel, C.: Detection of traffic signs in real-world images: the German traffic sign detection benchmark. In: The 2013 International Joint Conference on Neural Networks (IJCNN), pp. 1–8 (2013). https://doi.org/10.1109/IJCNN. 2013.6706807

13. Larsson, F., Felsberg, M.: Using fourier descriptors and spatial models for traffic sign recognition. In: Heyden, A., Kahl, F. (eds.) SCIA 2011. LNCS, vol. 6688, pp. 238–249. Springer, Heidelberg (2011). https://doi.org/10.1007/978-3-642-21227-7_23

14. Mogelmose, A., Trivedi, M.M., Moeslund, T.B.: Vision-based traffic sign detection and analysis for intelligent driver assistance systems: perspectives and survey. IEEE Trans. Intell. Transp. Syst. **13**(4), 1484–1497 (2012). https://doi.org/10.1109/TITS.2012.2209421

15. Aggar, A., Rahem, A.A., Zaiter, M.: Iraqi traffic signs detection based on YOLOv5. In: 2021 International Conference on Advanced Computer Applications (ACA), pp. 5–9 (2021). https://doi.org/10.1109/ACA52198.2021.9626821

16. Wang, C.Y., Mark Liao, H.Y., Wu, Y.H., Chen, P.Y., Hsieh, J.W., Yeh, I.H.: CSPNet. In: IEEE Computer Society Conference on Computer Vision and Pattern Recognition Workshops, vol. 2020-June, pp. 1571–1580 (2020)

17. Wang, K., Liew, J.H., Zou, Y., Zhou, D., Feng, J.: PANet: few-shot image semantic segmentation with prototype alignment. In: Proceedings of the IEEE International Conference on Computer Vision, vol. 2019-Octob, pp. 9196–9205 (2019). https://doi.org/10.1109/ICCV. 2019.00929

18. Goutte, C., Gaussier, E.: A probabilistic interpretation of Precision, Recall and F-Score, with implication for evaluation. In: Losada, D.E., Fernández-Luna, J.M. (eds.) ECIR 2005. LNCS, vol. 3408, pp. 345–359. Springer, Heidelberg (2005). https://doi.org/10.1007/978-3-540-31865-1_25

19. Intel Corporation: "Intel ® 64 and IA-32 Architectures Software Developer's Manual", Architecture, vol. 1, no. 253666, pp. 429–439 (2006). http://www.intel.com/design/itanium/man uals/iiasdmanual.htm

Prediction of the Arbutus Unedo Colonization Time via an Agent-Based Distribution Model

João Bioco[1,3]($\boxtimes$) (ID), Paula Prata[1,3] (ID), Fernando Cánovas[2] (ID), and Paulo Fazendeiro[1,3] (ID)

[1] Cloud Computing Competence Centre (C4-UBI), Universidade da Beira Interior, Covilhã, Portugal
joaobioco@gmail.com
[2] Facultad de Ciencias de la Salud, Universidad Católica San Antonio de Murcia, Murcia, Spain
[3] Instituto de Telecomunicações, Covilhã, Portugal

Abstract. Species distribution models (SDMs) have been used to predict the distribution of species in an environment. Usually, this prediction is based on previous species occurrence data. Nowadays, several species are facing climatic changes that impact the way species behave. Global warming has implicated species displacement from their natural habitat to new suitable places. SDMs can be used to anticipate possible impacts of the climatic changes in species distribution, preventing species extinction scenarios. New SDMs approaches are needed to give valuable information that better approximates these models to reality.

This paper presents a novel approach to the prediction of species distribution. It starts by using an agent-based model (ABM) to establish an approximate mapping between the geological and the computational times. Afterwards, the implemented ABM can be used to predict the species distribution at different time intervals.

The presented case study concerns the distribution of the *Arbutus unedo* in the Iberian peninsula, a species with relevant socio-economic impact in Portugal. The results show that the measurement of the geological time, supported by the approximate correspondence to the number of epochs of an ABM, can be a valuable tool for the prediction of the species distribution in a changing environmental scenario.

Keywords: Agent-based distribution model · Colonization time · Species distribution model

A species distribution model (SDM) describes the relationship between an environment constituted by a set of eco-geographical variables (EGVs) and the occurrence of a particular species by using a mathematical model [1,2]. Such methodology allows

This work was supported by operation Centro-01-0145-FEDER-000019 - C4 - Centro de Competências em Cloud Computing, cofinanced by the European Regional Development Fund (ERDF) through the Programa Operacional Regional do Centro (Centro 2020), in the scope of the Sistema de Apoio á Investigação Científica e Tecnológica - Programas Integrados de IC&DT. This work was also funded by FCT/MCTES through national funds and when applicable cofunded EU funds under the project UIDB/50008/2020 FCT/MCTES.

© ICST Institute for Computer Sciences, Social Informatics and Telecommunications Engineering 2023
Published by Springer Nature Switzerland AG 2023. All Rights Reserved
M. H. Miraz et al. (Eds.): iCETiC 2022, LNICST 463, pp. 107–117, 2023.
https://doi.org/10.1007/978-3-031-25161-0_8

a prediction of the spatial distribution for that species in different environmental scenarios. Several classical methods have been used to implement such SDMs [3–5], projecting the species habitat suitability that has a significant impact in the abundance and distribution of species [6,7]. These existing methods lack in projecting the distribution of species dynamically, in the sense that the previous distribution of the species in the study area, as well as the continuum changes in the environment from the initial environmental conditions until the environmental conditions of the projected period, are not considered. Therefore, classical species distribution models can omit crucial information about species' behavior.

The climate changes in nature, resulting in species extinction scenarios (animal and plants), have motivated the study of species distribution for management and preservation purposes and economic reasons [8,9].

In this work we present a novel approach to species distribution modeling that is accomplished by mapping the computational time, viz. epochs of an agent-based distribution model (ABM), and the geological time, which allows predicting the distribution of species over time in scenarios of heavy climatic changes. We choose as a case-study the distribution of the *A. unedo* in the Iberian Peninsula. Due to its socio-economical importance, information on how the species will spread in future environmental scenarios is essential for proper planning of forestation and reforestation actions.

Arbutus unedo is a plant species widespread in the Mediterranean region. Commonly known as strawberry tree, there are many derivatives of its fruit, such as the production of spirits drinks, the production of juice and yoghurt as well as the production of jam. It is also used in pastry, cosmetics, and nutrition medicine, among others [10] and is considered one of the major sources of revenue for Portuguese forestry owners [11]. Its benefits go beyond its fruit: the capacity of *A. unedo* to regenerate contributes to the conservation and rehabilitation of the soil [12]. Moreover *A. unedo* has noticeable environmental benefits: has a role in land recovery and desertification avoidance, contributes to maintain biodiversity, and may contribute to the discontinuity of the monocultures of pines and eucalypts, thus preventing the forest fire propagation [13].

1 Materials and Methods

For this study, an agent-based species distribution model was developed with the SDSim modelling tool [9] and applied to simulate the distribution of *A. unedo* in the Iberian Peninsula in two different geological periods, i.e., the Last Glacial Maximum (LGM, 10000 BP) and in the current period [14]. This agent-based species distribution model projects the suitability map of the species based on the relationship between the environment constituted by a set of EGVs and the species occurrence[1].

The suitability map represents the study area containing more and less suitable locations for the species' survival. Based on this suitability map, the distribution of the species is simulated following a defined species life cycle, consisting of three main phases: reproduction, death and spread. Constrained by the suitability value, the species occupation percentage at each location is increased based on a predefined birth rate;

---

[1] Alternatively, the ecologists can use their expertise regarding the mean optimal values, and standard deviation of each EGV considered suitable for the species.

then, the species occupation percentage reduces according to a death rate, and a percentage is transferred for the neighbouring locations according to a spread rate [9].

In agreement with the work presented in [11] nine EGVs that have the greater influence on the behaviour of *A. unedo* were selected: seven climatic variables ($BIO1$, $BIO2$, $BIO5$, $BIO9$, $BIO15$, t_{max}, t_{min}) from the WorldClim database 1.4 and two topographic variables (*slope* and *altitude*); altitude was obtained from the Global Multi-resolution Terrain Elevation Data 2010 [15]. The slope was generated from the altitude using the GDAL/OGR library [16]. Three simulation scenarios were performed by fixing the birth and death rates and varying the spread rate. Life cycle parameters were set up as follows: (*birth rate* $= 0.6$, *death rate* $= 0.2$, *spread rate* $= [0.2, 0.3, 0.4]$). Life cycle parameters were chosen according to our knowledge regarding the behavior of *A. unedo* in reproducing and spreading in suitable locations according to the current environmental conditions.

The approach for establishing a plausible approximation between each epoch of the agent-based model and the corresponding geological time consists of three main phases: 1) initialization; 2) estimation and 3) prediction. It is assumed that we have access to EGVs measured in two different, sufficiently far apart and distinct, moments in time[2].

In the initialization phase the distribution of the species is simulated in the past environmental conditions until a stable distribution of the species is observed. After that, this stable distribution of the species in the past is used to initialize the simulation of the species in the current environmental conditions. Usually, an abrupt change in the environmental conditions occurs, and the species distribution is simulated until the system reaches the stabilisation. The number of iterations needed to stabilise the distribution of the species in the current environmental conditions, *stabilisation_present*, is registered. Stabilisation is determined by the cell-by-cell comparison index [17].

In the estimation phase, the distribution of the species is simulated departing from the past to the current environmental conditions by linear interpolation of the EGVs. The initial number of bins for the interpolation, *itp_steps*, is fixed as the number of iterations necessary to stabilization after the harsh change of the previous phase, i.e. *stabilisation_present*. At each time step the environmental conditions change gradually approaching the current environmental conditions. From there, the EGVs are kept fixed and the simulation continues until stabilization. The number of iterations until stabilization after interpolation is denoted sTi. This is an induction process and in the next simulation, *itp_steps* is given by the sum of the previous *itp_steps* with the previous sTi. This procedure is repeated until sTi is less or equal than η (in the reported experiments $\eta = stabilisation\_present \times 0.05$).

Having completed this inductive interpolation process, we are finally in a position to hypothesise the quantification of each iteration into the corresponding geological time. The geological time g_{time} of each iteration of the agent-based computational model is approximated by the ratio between the geological time range and the total number of iterations until the final stabilisation of the system:

$$g_{time} = \Delta_T / itp\_steps, \tag{1}$$

---

[2] This notion of distance between the environmental conditions is inherently dependent on the species life-cycle. It suffices to think, for instance, that the notion of time has a very different meaning for trees and bacteria.

where Δ_T is the change over time, in the current case expressed in years, and itp_steps is the number of interpolation steps necessary to satisfy the defined condition. Note

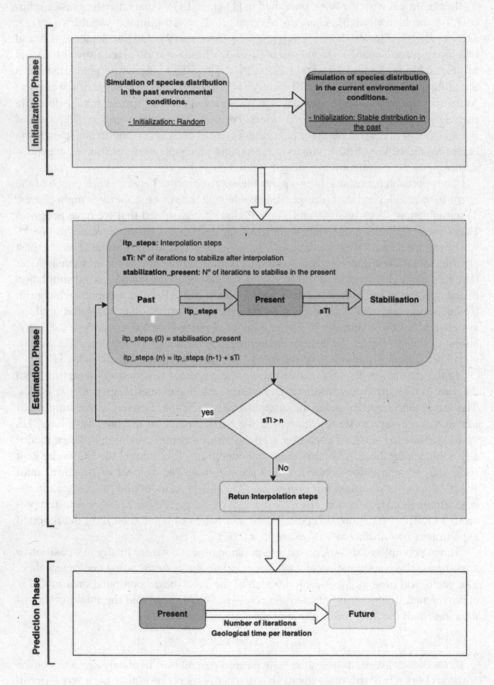

Fig. 1. Interpolation method

that this hypothesis depends on the assumption that environmental conditions vary uniformly and is also subjected to the constraints that the agent-based model has imposed on the species' life cycle. Finally, in the prediction phase, the information regarding the geological time is used to define the itp_steps needed to simulate the species distribution departing from the current to the future environmental conditions in a changing climatic scenario. Figure 1 describes the proposed approach from the initialization until the prediction phase.

2 Experiments and Results

2.1 Initialization and Estimation Phase

Figure 2(a) shows the suitability map of *A. unedo* in the past environmental conditions; and Fig. 2(b) shows the suitability map of *A. unedo* in the current environmental conditions. Comparing with the distribution of the species in the past, the chances for the *A. unedos'* survival are higher in the current environmental conditions. For example, temperature in the past was lower, limiting the species' growth. Some regions (in the west of the peninsula) have higher suitability values (greater than 0.8).

In contrast, in the past environmental conditions, the suitability values were lower (less than 0.5), limiting the chances of the species' survival, as confirmed in the past distribution map.

Figure 3(a) shows the distribution map of the species, resulting from the simulation in the past environmental conditions with the following life cycle parameters: birth rate = 0.6, death rate = 0.2 and spread rate = 0.4; and Fig. 3(b) shows the distribution map of the species in the current environmental conditions, using the same life cycle parameters.

Simulating the distribution of *A. unedo* in the past environmental conditions, 17 iterations were needed to stabilise, whereas, in the current environmental conditions, where the species has better conditions for reproducing and spreading, it took 270 iterations to stabilise.

Figure 4 shows the differences between two successive maps until the simulation stabilises. In the past environmental conditions where the initialisation of the species was random, differences between maps were higher at the beginning of the simulation. Then these differences decrease until the stop criterion is reached. Under the current environmental conditions, where the stable distribution of species in the past environmental conditions was used to initialise the species, these differences have lower values.

Figure 5 shows the order of the number of iterations needed to achieve stabilisation after each interpolation phase. For the scenarios of (birth rate: 0.6, death rate: 0.2, spread rate: 0.4) it took 3030 itp_steps until the stop criterion to be satisfied. For the scenarios of (birth rate: 0.6, death rate: 0.2, spread rate: 0.3) 3506 itp_steps were needed, and 3851 itp_steps for the scenarios of (birth rate: 0.6, death rate: 0.2, spread rate: 0.2).

2.2 Prediction Phase

Based on the proposed approach is in this case study, the distribution of *A. unedo* is simulated, departing from a stable distribution of the species in the current environmental conditions to the future environmental conditions (until 2070). According to the

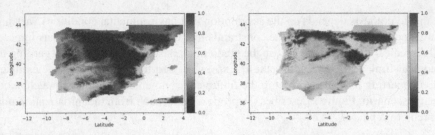

(a) Suitability Map of *A. unedo* in the past environmental conditions.

(b) Suitability Map of *A. unedo* in the current environmental conditions.

Fig. 2. Suitability map of *A. unedo* in the past and current environmental conditions.

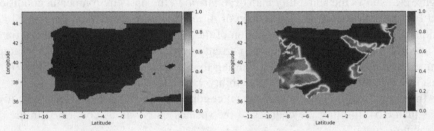

(a) Distribution Map of *A. unedo* in the past environmental conditions.

(b) Distribution Map of *A. unedo* in the current environmental conditions.

Fig. 3. Distribution Map of *A. unedo* in the past and current environmental conditions, using the following life cycle parameters - birth rate: 0.6, death rate: 0.2, spread rate: 0.4.

available data from WorldClim, current environmental conditions were collected from 1960 to 1990. For each EGV Worldclim calculates the average from 1960 to 1990. For this case study, we consider the start year of the prediction sequence, the year 1960. The future environmental conditions data were collected from WorldClim, in the rcp26 (representative concentration pathways) scenarios [18]. Assuming that geological time corresponding to one interpolation step (1 *itp_steps* or 1 iteration) is known, simulation performs by interpolating between current and future environmental conditions, i.e., changing the environmental conditions linearly.

Figure 6 shows the current suitability and future suitability map for *A. unedo* and the difference between these two maps (in absolute value); and also presents the current and future (the year 2070) distribution maps as well as the difference between these two maps (in absolute value).

In the predicted suitability map (Fig. 6(b)), some locations previously considered suitable in the current environmental conditions are less suitable. Some locations become even unsuitable for the species, whereas other locations considered unsuitable in the current environmental conditions become suitable for the species' survival.

From a stable distribution in the current environmental conditions to the future (2070), 33 *itp_steps* were needed.

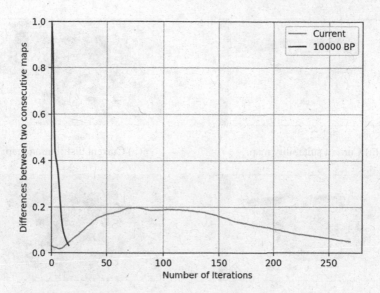

Fig. 4. Differences between two sequential maps in the past and present environmental conditions, using the following life cycle - birth rate: 0.6, death rate: 0.2, spread rate: 0.4.

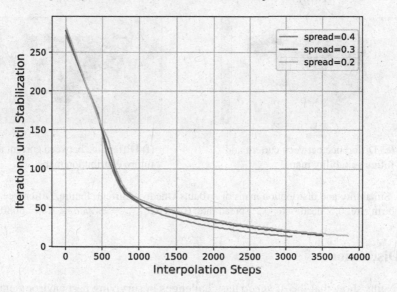

Fig. 5. Sequence of the number of iterations to reach stabilisation during the interpolation phase (birth rate: 0.6, death rate: 0.2).

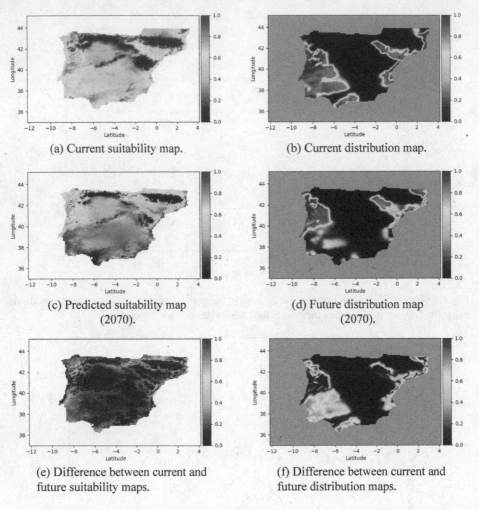

(a) Current suitability map.

(b) Current distribution map.

(c) Predicted suitability map (2070).

(d) Future distribution map (2070).

(e) Difference between current and future suitability maps.

(f) Difference between current and future distribution maps.

Fig. 6. Suitability and distribution maps of Arbutus Unedo - Current, Future, Difference. Parameters (birth rate: 0.6; death rate: 0.2; spread rate: 0.4; $1itp_{steps} = 3.3 years$; $its = 3030$).

3 Discussion

The results show that the *A. unedo* has challenges in surviving past environmental conditions. On the other hand, the current environmental conditions are more suitable for the species' survival.

The species' behaviour depends highly on suitability maps and the life cycle parameter values (birth rate, death rate and spread rate).

It is possible to verify that as the spread rate decreases, more time the simulation lasts until it reaches stabilisation, observing the three simulation scenarios (varying the spread to 0.2, 0.3, and 0.4). However, the three scenarios present similar patterns and behaviours. Initially, the number of iterations after the interpolation process (sTi) is considerably high. However, as the process is repeated, this number decreases until the stopping criteria of the simulation are satisfied, see Fig. 5.

Despite these similar patterns, there are differences in the number of iterations needed to stabilise the simulation in each scenario. Therefore, the amount of time needed for the species to spread until colonise is different in each simulation scenario, and its results depend considerably on the simulation parameters. For example, considering that the species spread less, one iteration at the computational level will correspond to a geological time unit inferior to the scenarios where the species spread more.

Table 1 presents the time per iteration for the *A. unedo*.

Table 1. Geological time corresponding to a single iteration of the agent-based model (time frame (Δ_T): 10.000 years).

Arbutus unedo (birth rate, death rate, spread rate)	Iteration until stabilisation	Time per iteration
(0.6, 0.2, 0.2)	3851	2.59 years
(0.6, 0.2, 0.3)	3506	2.85 years
(0.6, 0.2, 0.4)	3030	3.30 years

It is important to note that any results obtained are constrained by the life cycle parameters chosen and the model used to project the suitability maps of these species. Furthermore, this study assumes that environmental conditions change linearly from the LGM to the present. Another critical aspect of this study concerns the variation in the values of the environmental variables between the two-time points (LGM and present). If there is no significant variation between the values of the environmental variables in both time points, the interpolation phase is omitted.

According to the case study results, the suitability map of *A. unedo* will change in the future. Although these changes are not too significant, if considering only the predicted suitability map, see Fig. 6(c). Considering the distribution of species in a changing environment scenario and departing from a stable distribution in the current environmental conditions, the predicted distribution of the species for the year 2070 will be considerably different from the current distribution, see Fig. 6(f). In addition, the distribution of *A. unedo* in each year between the current and 2070 can be predicted. Predicting how species will spread over this period is possible if one knows the mapping between computational and geological time. Knowledge of the temporal mapping could be sufficient to simulate the number of iterations corresponding to the geological time to be analysed.

4   Concluding Remarks

This study improves the techniques used in species distribution models by proposing a constructive method to determine the species' geological time to colonisation, allowing the prediction of the species distribution in continuum time in a changing environmental scenario, different from the others approaches that predict species distribution considering only the environmental conditions of the period of interest. A direct application can be found in predicting the distribution of species over time in climate change scenarios. The proposed approach can serve as a starting point for a more realistic analysis of species behaviour. The idea is to get a matching as good as possible between the computational time (epochs of an agent-based model) and the geological time. With this information at hand we foresee that it is possible to predict more accurately the response of a species to an expected future environmental change predicted to occur in a precise moment of the chronological timeline.

References

1. Meynard, C.N., Leroy, B., Kaplan, D.M.: Testing methods in species distribution modelling using virtual species: what have we learnt and what are we missing? Ecography **42**(12), 2021–2036 (2019)
2. Araújo, M.B., New, M.: Ensemble forecasting of species distributions. Trends Ecol. Evol. **22**(1), 42–47 (2007)
3. Phillips, S.J., Anderson, R.P., Schapire, R.E.: Maximum entropy modeling of species geographic distributions. Ecol. Model. **190**(3–4), 231–259 (2006)
4. Elith, J., et al.: Novel methods improve prediction of species' distributions from occurrence data. Ecography **29**(2), 129–151 (2006)
5. Golding, N., August, T.A., Lucas, T.C., Gavaghan, D.J., van Loon, E.E., McInerny, G.: The zoon r package for reproducible and shareable species distribution modelling. Methods Ecol. Evol. **9**(2), 260–268 (2018)
6. Sporbert, M., et al.: Testing macroecological abundance patterns: the relationship between local abundance and range size, range position and climatic suitability among european vascular plants. J. Biogeogr. **47**(10), 2210–2222 (2020)
7. Margalef-Marrase, J., Pérez-Navarro, M.Á., Lloret, F.: Relationship between heatwave-induced forest die-off and climatic suitability in multiple tree species. Glob. Change Biol. **26**(5), 3134–3146 (2020)
8. Bioco, J., Fazendeiro, P., Cánovas, F., Prata, P.: Parameterization of an agent-based model of spatial distribution of species. In: Miraz, M.H., Excell, P.S., Ware, A., Soomro, S., Ali, M. (eds.) iCETiC 2020. LNICST, vol. 332, pp. 251–260. Springer, Cham (2020). https://doi.org/10.1007/978-3-030-60036-5_18
9. Bioco, J., Cánovas, F., Prata, P., Fazendeiro, P.: SDSim: a generalized user friendly web ABM system to simulate spatiotemporal distribution of species under environmental scenarios. Environ. Modell. Softw. **147**, 105234 (2022). https://www.sciencedirect.com/science/article/pii/S1364815221002760
10. Notícias, D.D.: O medronho que o fogo levou, August 2018. https://www.dn.pt/pais/medronho-9700495.html. Accessed 30 Apr 2022
11. Ribeiro, M.M., et al.: Bioclimatic modeling in the last glacial maximum, mid-holocene and facing future climatic changes in the strawberry tree (arbutus unedo l.). PLOS One **14**(1), 1–15 (2019). https://doi.org/10.1371/journal.pone.0210062
12. Mesléard, F., Lepart, J.: Continuous basal sprouting from a lignotuber: arbutus unedo l. anderica arborea l., as woody mediterranean examples. Oecologia **80**(1), 127–131 (1989)
13. Gomes, M.F.F.N.: Strategies for the improvement of Arbutus unedo L. (strawberry tree): in vitro propagation, mycorrhization and diversity analysis. Ph.D. thesis, Universidade de Coimbra (Portugal) (2011)

14. Hijmans, R.J., Cameron, S.E., Parra, J.L., Jones, P.G., Jarvis, A.: Very high resolution inter-polated climate surfaces for global land areas. Int. J. Climatol. J. Roy. Meteorol. Soc. **25**(15), 1965–1978 (2005)

15. Danielson, J.J., Gesch, D.B.: Global multi-resolution terrain elevation data 2010 (GMTED2010). US Department of the Interior, US Geological Survey (2011)

16. GDAL/OGR contributors: GDAL/OGR Geospatial Data Abstraction software Library. Open Source Geospatial Foundation (2022). https://gdal.org

17. Kuhnert, M., Voinov, A., Seppelt, R.: Comparing raster map comparison algorithms for spatial modeling and analysis. Photogram. Eng. Remote Sens. **71**(8), 975–984 (2005)

18. Van Vuuren, D.P., et al.: The representative concentration pathways: an overview. Clim. Change **109**(1), 5–31 (2011)

Stock Price Prediction Using Semi-supervised Ridge Regression

Muhammed J. A. Patwary[1] , Md. Jahedul Karim[1] , Sakib Iqram Hamim[1] ,
Mohammed Sifath[1] , Mohammad Arif Sobhan Bhuiyan[2] ,
and Mahdi H. Miraz[2(✉)]

[1] International Islamic University Chittagong, Chittagong, Bangladesh
[2] Xiamen University Malaysia, Sepang, Malaysia
`arifsobhan.bhuiyan@xmu.edu.my`, `m.miraz@ieee.org`

Abstract. Stock price prediction is the technique of predicting the future values
of a stocks or other financial instruments traded on any exchange. Stock price
prediction using machine learning approaches has become very polular in the past
few years. Different scholars and researchers have studied and suggested different
types of stock price prediction models, most of which was based on supervised
learning. Semi-supervised based models in this regard are in fact less explored.
In this paper, we developed a machine learning model using semi-supervised
self-training method with ridge regression to predict stock price. Semi-supervised
learning takes advantage of both labelled and unlabelled data. While the historical
data of the stocks were used in the taining dataset, the daily close prices of the
stocks were taken as prediction targets. In this approach, we first begin by obtaining the labelled data instances from a dataset that comprises both labelled and
unlabelled data. Utilising the labelled training data, a regression algorithm was
trained and the unlabelled data were predicted. This newly labelled data is called
'pseudo-labelled' data, which is then concatenated with the train data to retrain
this model. Thus the process was iterated several times until the best performance
is achieved. With a 98% prediction accuracy, using fewer instances, the model
demonstrated significant improvement compared to the reported performances of
other existing models.

Keywords: Stock price prediction · Semi-supervised · Self-training · Ridge
regression

1 Introduction

Stock price prediction is the technique of predicting the future values of stocks or other
financial instruments traded on any exchange. At stock markets, both individual and
institutional investors come together to pur-chase and sell shares in a public venue.
Stock price movements are difficult to forecast since they are heavily impacted by political information and economic developments in the global markets [1]. By predicting
stock prices, the investors foresee the future values to be traded on an exchange. With

© ICST Institute for Computer Sciences, Social Informatics and Telecommunications Engineering 2023
Published by Springer Nature Switzerland AG 2023. All Rights Reserved
M. H. Miraz et al. (Eds.): iCETiC 2022, LNICST 463, pp. 118–128, 2023.
https://doi.org/10.1007/978-3-031-25161-0_9

accurate prediction of the stock prices, we can reduce the risk of the investors. By aiding to understand when and where and how to invest (buy and sell), can help to maximise their return on investment (ROI). Precisely predicting the stock prices is very difficult due to the involvement and influences of various factors which makes stock prices dynamic and volatile. However, with recent advances in computing technology, the stock prices can now be predicted more accurately [2]. The semi-supervised app-roach is regarded as one of the promising strategies in machine learning research [3, 4]. It combines the benefits of both supervised and unsupervised approaches to develop a novel learning method [5, 6]. A little amount of labelled data with unlabelled data is used in semi-supervised approaches, which reduces the expense of collecting labelled data. The concept of semi-supervised approaches was first developed in 1965 by Scud-der [7]. It has recently emerged as one of the most important machine learning and data mining approaches [8]. It is defined as a strategy that combines supervised and unsuper-vised learning. We used the self-training method in our model, which is an important semi-supervised algorithm. Self-training is one of the initial semi-supervised techniques. Training the classifier with the help of a few labelled data, this classifier is used to sort through a large amount of unlabelled data. Ridge regression, initially proposed by Hoerl and Kennard [9] in 1970, is now a renowned parameter estimation strategy to cope with the correlation issue that regularly occurs in multiple linear regression research. The correlation between linearly independent variables is strong in ridge regression.

One of the main aims of this study is to predict stock prices with the help of the SSRR model as well as to observe the stock closed prices for any stock index. How the stock market will react in the future can also be predicted. Much research has been conducted on stock market prediction using supervised models, whereas research on stock price prediction using semi-supervised models is comparatively less focused. In most of the supervised model, it has been observed that there is significant mismatch between the original price and the predicted price. Therefore, we used a semi-supervised self-training with a ridge regression (SSRR) based model to minimise the error rate and improve the prediction accuracy [10].

We developed a machine learning model, which is a semi-supervised self-training method with ridge regression (SSRR), to forecast the stock price. In this model we train the regressor by a few labelled data and predict the remaining unlabelled data as an output. Thus we get 'pseudo-labelled' data which is then combined with the labelled train data to retrain the regressor. After pre-defined iterations (i.e. 100), we get the expected result.

This research study's key contribution is to implement the semi-supervised self-training algorithm to predict stock index prices and increase the prediction accuracy. A small amount of labelled data is used to train the classifier then the large amount of unlabelled data labelled using the self-training classifier. The classifier was converted into a regressed method to predict the accuracy of the stock price using ridge regression. Our proposed methodology for the stock index price prediction outperforms other semi-supervised models.

The rest of the article is organised as follows: Sect. 2 summarises the previous related researches and also discusses our suggested approach, which is a semi-supervised learning technique based on ridge regression; the results and discussion are explained in Sect. 3 and finally Sect. 4 concludes the article and states future research directions.

2 Related Works

Since the beginning of stock markets, many research have been conducted and numerous models have been created to predict the stock index prices. Many scholars have created numerous models of stock market prediction in recent years, such as:

Zhu et al. [11] used Support Vector Machine (SVM) and Gaussian Bayesian classification methods to predict the stock index. The classification goal was to determine whether the stock price or index would rise or fall at the following trading day. The Principal Component Analysis (PCA) was also used to reduce data redundancy and the dimensions of the index of classification characteristics. The prediction efficiency improved after the use of Principal Component Analysis. A comparison between PCA-SVM and PCA Gaussian Bayes was made; PCA-SVM has been found to be significantly better than PCA-Gaussian Bayes. Without PCA, the prediction efficiency of SVM and Gaussian Bayes were comparatively much lower. As a result, it can be concluded from their research that the machine learning model's classification prediction performance was greatly enhanced following the data dimension reduction.

Kia et al. [12] extended the work of Park and Shin [13] and proposed a hybrid model to forecast next-day movement of global stock markets, in which graph-based semi-supervised label spreading algorithm and a supervised SVM model were combined. The graph-based semi-supervised model was developed with a novel continuous Kruskal-based graph construction algorithm whereas the supervised model was rather developed with simple SVM. The capacity of graph-based semi-supervised algorithms to use global market data for forecasting is determined by the network that is built to describe market interaction. By combining global market data with historical data from the markets to be forecasted, a more accurate forecast can be made.

Zhang et al. [14] proposed a Generative Adversarial Network (GAN) architecture with an Long Short-term Memory (LSTM) network as the generator for predicting the stock closing price and Multi-Layer Perceptron (MLP) as the discriminator. By providing stock data from several previous days, the model was trained using an end-to-end manner to forecast the daily closing price of the stock. Instead of relying solely on classic regression approaches to predict prices, they generated the same distributions of the daily stock data through the adversarial learning system. The dataset of the SP 500 Index, Shanghai Composite Index, IBM from the New York Stock Exchange (NYSE) and Microsoft Corporation (MSFT) from NASDAQ was collected from Yahoo finance. The GAN architecture showed better results in predicting the closing price on real data compared with some other models.

Pang et al. [15] created a novel neural network approach to improve stock market forecasting. For real-time and offline analysis, data were gathered from a livestock exchange. To forecast the stock market, they developed a deep long short-term memory (LSTM) neural network with an embedded layer and a long short-term memory neural network with an automated encoder. In this experiment, the deep LSTM with an embedded layer slightly outperformed the LSTM with automated encoder. While the accuracy of the deep LSTM was 57.2%, that of the LSTM neural network with an automated encoder was 56.9%.

Mehta *et al.* [16] used various models, namely autoregressive integrated moving average (ARIMA), LSTM, and Linear Regression, to forecast stock prices. In addition, sentiment analysis was performed on tweets about the firm or the stock. The dataset is collected from Yahoo finance. The accuracy of the ARIMA model was better than the LSTM and Linear Regression because, for prediction, it just uses the current window unlike the other two models, using the past or historical data for prediction.

For many years, machine learning algorithms and linear approaches have been studied with the goal of developing reliable prediction models. Deep learning models have recently been recognised as emerging technologies in this domain. Jiang [17] conducted a survey on the recent research and development in deep learning models for stock market prediction. In fact, only a few research used semi-supervised learning to forecast the model while most of them utilised supervised learning methods. There are many hybrid models with neural networks where recurrent neural network (RNN) and convolutional neural network (CNN), are mostly used.

Yang *et al.* [18] developed a deep neural network ensemble model, known as multilayer feedforward neural networks, to forecast the Chinese stock market index on the basis of the most recent input indices. Shanghai composite index and Shenzhen Stock Exchange (SZSE) component index are top two amongst the Chinese stock market indices [19]. Historical data of these markets were used to train the network by Adam algorithm and Backpropagation. The bagging method combined these two networks to create an ensemble to lower the error of generalisation. The prediction accuracy of the 'high' and 'low' attributes were satisfactory, however, the 'close' attribute did not demonstrate satisfactory result using this method.

Pahwa *et al.* [20] proposed a novel model utilising a machine learning algorithm to forecast future stock prices. Linear regression, a simple classifier, has been used in this model. The algorithm can be optimised using Gradient Descent, Batch Learning, and Constrained Methods. The result is entirely based on numbers and it is predicated on a number of axioms that can or can't hold in the real world, such as forecasting time. The SVM can be a well-supervised machine learning algorithm in replacement of the used methods.

David *et al.* [21] introduced a three phased stock market forecasting systems. Multiple Regression Analysis, Type-2 Fuzzy Clustering and Fuzzy type-2 Neural Network are the three phases of this system. The three phases were combined to form this hybrid model. To develop the forecasting model, Type-2 Fuzzy Clustering was used. The comparison between the Fuzzy type-1 technique and the Fuzzy type-2 technique was shown in the forecasting system while a Fuzzy type-2 technique was employed instead of a Fuzzy type-1 technique. This has thus resulted in the reduction of the prediction errors. The proposed approach outperforms the existing established methods for predicting stock market values, according to the findings of the research.

2.1 Semi-supervised Learning

In a semi-supervised approach, both labelled and unlabelled data can be utilised to attain better performance. We can achieve good performance using only fewer labelled instances. This technique reduces the complexity as well as minimises the cost.

2.2 Ridge Regression

In 1970, Hoerl and Kennard [9] initially proposed the Ridge regression theory. Ridge regression is a regularisation approach for linear regression models that helps them perform effectively in instances when the data used to train the model has a lot of volatility. If there are several factors, ridge regression is the best option [22]. In fact, it performs better when there are a lot of predictors, each with a little impact. Ridge regression removes the coefficients of linear regression, where variables are interrelated and there exist a lot of variations. We used ridge regression to avoid overfitting in our training dataset. By changing the parameter (lambda), Ridge regression solves the multicollinearity problem. In Multi-Linear-Regression, we know that,

$$y = \beta_0 + \beta_1 x_1 + \beta_2 x_2 + \ldots\ldots\ldots\ldots + \beta_n x_n \tag{1}$$

$$y_i = \beta_0 + \sum \beta_i x_i \tag{2}$$

$$\sum y_i - \beta_0 - \sum \beta_i x_i$$

Cost/Loss function

$$\sum \{y_i - \beta_0 - \sum \beta_i x_{ij}\}^2 \tag{3}$$

Regularised term

$$\lambda \sum \beta_i^2 \tag{4}$$

$$Ridge\ Regression\ =\ Loss\ function\ +\ Regularised\ term \tag{5}$$

Putting Eq. 3 and Eq. 4 in Eq. 5 RidgeRegression =

$$\sum y_i - \beta_0 - \sum \beta_i x_{ij} 2 + \lambda \sum \beta_i^2 \tag{6}$$

Here,
  x_0, x_1...x_n is an independent variable:
  y_0, y_1...y_n is the target variable.
  β is coefficients.
  λ is the penalty-factor.

2.3 Self-training

One of several semi-supervised strategies is the self-training. In the semi-supervised self-training approach, a very little amount of labelled data are used to train a classifier and a prediction is made based on the unlabelled data using the classifier [23]. Prediction with self-training is significantly better than random guessing. Data predicted by the classifier is adopted as the "pseudo-labelled" data in a subsequent iterations of the classifier. This semi-supervised technique is called self-training.

Algorithm 1. Self-Training Algorithm

---
1. Train the model with labelled training data set a1, b1
2. Predict unlabelled data where $a \in a_u$
3. Concatenate (a, x(a)) with labelled data.
4. Iterate until model prediction is satisfied.

Algorithm 2. Proposed Algorithm (SSRR).

0: **while** $(U_d! = empty)$ and$(I \leq MAX)$ **do**
0: $N=1$;
0: R will train by L_d
0: **for** each a_i in U_d **do**
0: Give a_i a pseudo-label based on the prediction accuracy.
0: **end for**
0: Store a set of P_d of predictions from U_d.
0: Update $I= I+1; L_d= L_d \cup P_d$;
0: **end while**
Output: All labeled dataset.
0: $=0$

Here,

I: iteration Number; R: regressor; Ld: Labelled data; Ud: Unlabelled data; MAX: maximum number of iterations.

We divided the labelled data set into training and test data sets. We have then trained the regressor model with the labelled training data set. The unlabelled data is then predicted using the trained regressor model. These predicted unlabelled data are then used as 'pseudo-labels' data, without considering the probability. We added the labelled training data with the 'pseudo label' data and retrained our regressor model with this combined data set. In the next step, we predicted the close price for the labelled test data. We have then evaluated the regressor performance. Thus, steps 1 through steps 4 were iterated 100 times, until we get the required result.

3   Results and Discussion

The dataset Apple (AAPL) stock data, collected from the Yahoo finance data warehouse, was used to predict the stock price (Table 1).

Table 1. Dataset details

Data type:	Continuous
Task	Regression
Attribute type	Continuous
Area	Financial Area
Number of instances	10407
Number of attributes	07

After completing the necessary procedures, we ran the experiment to verify whether the provided approach was enough and also examined the correlation with the attributes: Low, Open, Volume, High, Close, and Adjusted Close, as shown in Fig. 1.

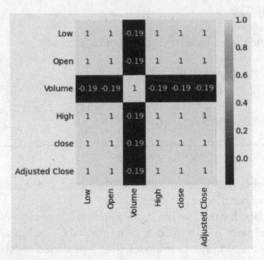

Fig. 1. Examining the correlation with the features

Figure 2 illustrates how close prices change over the time. It can be seen that the close prices move equally from 0 to 6500 data, however, after 6500 data, the close price significantly changes.

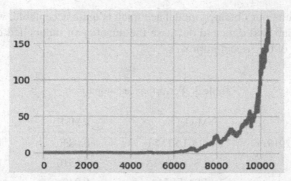

Fig. 2. Change in close price over the time

Table 2. Model evaluation

Iteration	Test RMSE	Accuracy score
1/10	0.015000282961063635	0.9821161882448355
2/10	0.015000282961063227	0.9821161882448364
3/10	0.015000282961063755	0.9821161882448352
4/10	0.015000282961064267	0.9821161882448339
5/10	0.015000282961067566	0.982116188244826
6/10	0.015000282961067648	0.9821161882448258
7/10	0.015000282961072768	0.9821161882448137
8/10	0.015000282961073811	0.9821161882448112
9/10	0.015000282961074451	0.9821161882448096
10/10	0.015000282961081367	0.9821161882447932

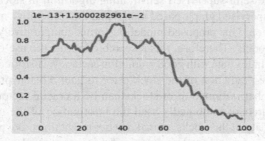

Fig. 3. Change in RMSE at various iterations

Table 2 shows the test RMSE with an accuracy score. Here we only showed the first ten iterations of our model. As seen in Fig. 3, after the 40th iteration the test RMSE started to slightly decreas, however, it rapidly kept declining after the 60th iteration, whereas accuracy score kept increasingd. According to the provided data using the proposed algorithm, our obtained model accuracy is quite acceptable, which is 98%. If we increase the labelled data and decrease the quantity of unlabelled data in our data set, the accuracy of the model improves.

Table 3. Performance comparison

Researchers	Model	RMSE	MSE
Chung and Shin (2018)	GA-LSTM	0.0836	0.007
Zhang (2017)	CSO-ARMA	0.0316	0.001
Hegazy (2015)	FPA-ELM	0.2400	0.0576
Rout (2014)	PSO-Elman	0.0632	0.004
Proposed	SSRR	0.0150	0.0002

Table 3 compares the performance of our proposed method with other already reported approached. Overall, our datasets in the proposed model produces comparatively superior results. The final accuracy is also good. The results may differ based on the size of the different datasets. We set the iteration level at 100. The error rate gradually decreases after a specific number of iterations.

4   Conclusions

We developed a semi-supervised ridge regression (SSRR) based model to forecast the stock index price of a stock market. The self-training classifier was converted using simple ridge regression to predict the time series data of the stock index prices. While there are many supervised models utilised in various research, only a few semi-supervised models were developed for stock price prediction. To the best of our knowledge, we are pioneer in using the semi-supervised self-training algorithm in stock price prediction. In the past, semi-supervised graph-based model and the Generative model were used in stock price prediction. Our proposed model performs comparatively better than other semi-supervised models. Therefore, this research confirms the use of the self-training algorithms in stock index data with good prediction accuracy. Historical data of the stocks are important in the prediction of the stock price to gain a better prediction accuracy. In addition, the global information of stocks can be a crucial factor for this purpose. In fact, many researchers combinedly used the information of the global stocks price with the historical data of the stocks, to make better predictions. We plan to enhance the data set in the future and construct an enhanced semi-supervised model for forecasting stock index prices. Fuzziness-based semi-supervised machine learning method can be considered in this regard.

References

1. Zhang, J., Cui, S., Xu, Y., Li, Q., Li, T.: A novel data-driven stock price trend prediction system. Expert Syst. Appl. **97**, 60–69 (2018)
2. Ehsan, H., Haratizadeh, S.: CNNpred: CNN-based stock market prediction using a diverse set of variables. Expert Syst. Appl. **129**, 273–285 (2019)
3. Faisal, M. F., et al.: Credit approval system using machine learning: challenges and future directions. In: 2021 International Conference on Computing, Networking, Telecommunications Engineering Sciences Applications (CoNTESA) (2021)
4. Patwary, M.J., Akter, S., Alam, M.B., Karim, A.R.: Bank deposit prediction using ensemble learning. Artif. Intell. Evol., 42–51, (2021)
5. Patwary, M.J.A., Wang, X.Z.: Sensitivity analysis on initial classifier accuracy in fuzziness based semi-supervised learning. Inf. Sci. **490**, 93–112 (2019)
6. Karim, S., Akter, N., Patwary, M.J.A.: Predicting autism spectrum disorder (ASD) meltdown using fuzzy semi- supervised learning with NNRW. In: 2022 International Conference on Innovations in Science, Engineering and Technology (ICISET) (2022)
7. Scudder, H.: Probability of error of some adaptive pattern-recognition machines. IEEE Trans. Inf. Theory **11**(3), 363–371 (1965)
8. Osman, A.B., et al.: Examining mental disorder/psychological chaos through various ML and DL techniques: a critical review. Ann. Emerg. Technol. Comput. (AETiC), 61–71 (2022)
9. Hoerl, A.E., Kennard, R.W.: Ridge regression: applications to non-orthogonal problems. Technometrics **12**(1), 69–82 (1970)
10. Patwary, M.J., Cao, W., Wang, X.Z., Haque, M.A.: Fuzziness based semi-supervised multi-modal learning for patient's activity recognition using RGBDT videos. Appl. Soft Comput. **120**, 108655 (2022)
11. Zhu, S., Zhao, M., Wei, S., An, S.: Stock index prediction based on principal component analysis and machine learning. In: 2020 International Conference on Big Data Artificial Intelligence Software Engineering (ICBASE), pp. 246–249 (2020)
12. Kia, A.N., Haratizadeh, S., Shouraki, S.B.: A hybrid supervised semi-supervised graph-based model to predict oneday ahead movement of global stock markets and commodity prices. Expert Syst. Appl. **105**, 159–173 (2018)
13. Park, K., Shin, H.: Stock price prediction based on a complex interrelation network of economic factors. Eng. Appl. Artif. Intell. **26**(5–6), 1550–1561 (2013)
14. Zhang, K., Zhong, G., Dong, J., Wang, S., Wang, Y.: Stock market prediction based on generative adversarial network. Procedia Comput. Sci. **147**, 400–406 (2019)
15. Pang, X., Zhou, Y., Wang, P., Lin, W., Chang, V.: An innovative neural network approach for stock market prediction. J. Supercomput. **76**(3), 2098–2118 (2018). https://doi.org/10.1007/s11227-017-2228-y
16. Mehta, Y., Malhar, A., Shankarmani, R.: Stock price prediction using machine learning and sentiment analysis. In: 2021 2nd International Conference for Emerging Technology (INCET) (2021)
17. Jiang, W.: Applications of deep learning in stock market prediction: recent progress. Expert Syst. Appl. **184**, 115537 (2021)
18. Yang, B., Gong, Z.J., Yang, W.: Stock market index prediction using deep neural network ensemble. In: 2017 36th Chinese Control Conference (ccc) (2017)
19. Han, C., Wang, Y., Xu, Y.: Efficiency and multifractality analysis of the Chinese stock market: evidence from stock indices before and after the 2015 stock market crash. Sustainability **11**(6), 1699 (2019)
20. Pahwa, K., Agarwal, N.: Stock market analysis using supervised machine learning. In: 2019 International Conference on Machine Learning, Big Data, Cloud and Parallel Computing (COMITCon) (2019)

21. Enke, D., Grauer, M., Mehdiyev, N.: Stock market prediction with multiple regression, fuzzy type-2 clustering and neural networks. Procedia Comput. Sci. **6**, 201–206 (2011)

22. Algamal, Z.Y.: Shrinkage parameter selection via modified cross-validation approach for ridge regression model. Commun. Stat.-Simul. Comput. **49**(7), 1922–1930 (2020)

23. Alam, M.S.B., Patwary, M.J.A., Hassan, M.: Birth mode prediction using bagging ensemble classifier: a case study of bangladesh. In: 2021 International Conference on Information and Communication Technology for Sustainable Development (ICICT4SD) (2021)

Accessibility of Multimedia Resources from Irish Universities for People with Epilepsy

Mohammed Fakrudeen(✉)

Higher College of Technology, Abu Dhabi, UAE
mrahim@hct.ac.ae

Abstract. The young People with Epilepsy (PwE) felt difficulty accessing the video content due to flashes and flickering. Universities failed to check the accessibility of videos before posting them on their websites or YouTube channel. In this research, the accessibility of video for PwE is explored. The study was conducted with 42 video clips posted by the top fourteen Irish universities ranked by Webometrics. For each university, three video clips were extracted from the YouTube channel posted by respective universities. Then, the video was analyzed with the Photosensitive Epilepsy Analysis Tool (PEAT). The number of warnings, luminance flash failures, red flash failures, and passed/failed results were recorded for each video sample. Among the fourteen universities, only one university achieve given above 50%. Seven universities failed in all samples. The remaining six universities achieve success below 50%. Out of 42 primary videos, eight videos didn't accept any luminance flash failures. Seventy-three percent of the samples don't have red flash failures implying university videos are less dangerous for red flashes. To achieve an adequate level of multimedia resources and to create inclusive videos, it is suggested to combine the evaluation methods with the PEAT tool and request a manual revision with Web Content Accessibility Guidelines (WCAG).

Keywords: Multimedia resources · Video · Higher education · Accessibility · Flashes

1 Introduction

Epilepsy is a neurological condition in which the brain activity becomes distorted, causing unusual behavior or seizure, sensations, and loss of awareness. Epilepsy is more frequent in elderly people and children, although it can strike anyone at any age.. Epilepsy is a complex disease with different risk factors. By and large, epilepsy has a solid hereditary inclination, as opposed to a condition with solitary reason and a solitary articulation. Comorbidities are increasingly being recognized as important common etiological and prognostic indicators. Epilepsy is significant trouble regarding personal satisfaction, bleakness, and danger of untimely mortality, particularly in individuals who keep on having seizures. Understanding the etiology of seizures can help avoid epilepsy [1].

M. H. Miraz et al. (Eds.): iCETiC 2022, LNICST 463, pp. 129–140, 2023.
https://doi.org/10.1007/978-3-031-25161-0_10

Epilepsy represents a vast extent of the world's disease trouble, influencing around 50 million individuals worldwide. An expected 5,000,000 individuals are determined to have epilepsy every year. In high-income countries, there are estimated to be 49 people diagnosed with epilepsy for every 100,000 people. In low-and middle-income nations, this figure can be as high as 139 for each 100 000. This is most likely due to the increased risk of endemic conditions, such as intestinal sickness or neurocysticercosis; the higher rate of street traffic injuries; birth-related grievances; and assortments in clinical infrastructure, accessible care, and accessibility preventive wellbeing programs. Near 80% of individuals with epilepsy live in low and middle-income nations [2].

In Ireland, 1 in 115 people has epilepsy. More than 10,000 are children, and 10,000 are women of childbearing age. In Ireland, 37,000 individuals over five years old have epilepsy. There are an expected 1,300 - 2,100 new analyses each year. Epilepsy Ireland gauges that there are 10,000 - 15,000 individuals in Ireland living with uncontrolled seizures. Awareness of the cause and symptoms is significantly less [3].

The web is rapidly becoming a non-debatable necessity and a crucial piece of the enlightening experience. Suppose the guarantee of all-inclusive access, which is vital to Berners-Lee's vision, is not met. In that case, many individuals may be denied the opportunity to achieve their educational and career ambitions [4].

A few people are vulnerable to seizures brought about by flashing, flickering and strobing effects. This sort of seizure is some of the time alluded to as a photo epileptic seizure since it is brought about by a pulse of light intermingling with the body's focal sensory system and the eye's light-responsive neurons.

Most web content is innocuous to people with photo epileptic inclinations. Indeed, the vast majority of films, animations, and Flash content pose no hazard. However, a few developers demand emotional impacts of glimmering or flickering lights and strobe-like impacts. Horror film sneak peeks, modest-looking pennant advertisements and Sci-fi style flash materials are among the awful lawbreakers. Possibly the makers of these impacts believe they are "cool," yet they are additionally possibly perilous [5].

In Ireland, some of the universities follow University Act 1997, the Employment Equality Act 1998–2004, the Disability Act 2005, and Equal Status Acts 2000–2004 to make educational content accessible to all [6]. However, for effective university marketing strategies and to provide information about the university to the student who seeks admission, the accessibility standards are not maintained.

Thus, the current research focuses on the accessibility of multimedia resources predominantly on videos that provide information about their institutions. In this exploration, the WCAG 2.1 was applied to decide whether the substance of the videos surveyed meets the requirements or not. It is fundamental to realize the data identified with educational recordings, for example, size, length, and design. The evidence serves as an input to break down the video with the is PEAT[1] developed by the University of Maryland Trace Center. As a contextual investigation, the current study took forty-two videos taken arbitrarily from the sites of the top fourteen universities in Ireland as per Webometrics[2].

---

[1] https://trace.umd.edu/peat.

[2] https://www.webometrics.info/en/Europe/Ireland%20.

The WCAG criteria for video flash and flickering were investigated in Sect. 2 of this study. Section 3 demonstrates the data extraction and analysis method. Section 4 examines the obtained data using a variety of parameters that affect the video's brightness. The study's findings are analyzed and implications are drawn in Sect. 5. Finally, the study offered specific recommendations and opportunities for improving video accessibility.

2 Background

Seizures brought about by light are known as photosensitive epilepsy. Photosensitive epilepsy can be activated by the substance that flashes, glints, or flickers. Web advancements that utilize animations, videos, canvas, and JavaScript movement are equipped for instigating seizures. If there should be an occurrence of photosensitive epilepsy, seizures are activated by flashing lights [7].

The Epilepsy Foundation gives a rundown of triggers that may cause seizures in photosensitive individuals [8]:

- Computer screens or TV screens because of glimmer or moving pictures,
- Intense strobe lights like visual alarms, and
- Certain visual forms, particularly stripes of differentiating hues.

World Wide Web Consortium(W3C) differentiates the flash and flickering. It characterizes flickering as an interruption issue, while flashing alludes to content that occurs more than 3 times per second which is huge and brilliant enough. NASA takes note that flickering and flashing are significant devices to draw attention. In this way, it is vital to comprehend that all flashes and flickering are not risky [9].

The Epilepsy Foundation of America expresses that "A flash is a potential risk if it has luminance at any rate 20 cd/m2, happens at a recurrence of least 3 Hz, and involves a strong visual edge of in any event 0.006 steradians (about 10% of the focal visual field or 25% of screen territory at typical viewing distances)" [10]. Thus, WCAG 2.3.1 general flash and red flash thresholds are defined as follows [11]:

According to PEAT [12], "The combined area of flashes occurring concurrently occupies no more than a total of one-quarter of any 341 x 256-pixel rectangle anywhere on the displayed screen area when the content is viewed at 1024 by 768 pixels".

A red flash is still another essential burn that extinguishes the accessibility of video. Saturated Red is a rare, dangerous condition, and there is special testing for it. Despite a red scenario having an impact on persons with traumatic brain injury's cognitive abilities, a red range's frequency seems to call for special attention and unusual examinations. [13] noticed that the seizure rates were a lot higher than anticipated due to red flashes when testing using the PEAT.

PEAT created by The Trace Research and Development Center assists to decide if the animations or video in their substance are probably going to cause seizures. PEAT is free downloadable software suggested by W3C. PEAT is talentcd in detecting general flash failures, red flash failures, and expanded flash warnings [12]. PEAT disallows to survey the material industrially created for gaming, home entertainment, or television broadcast. Nonetheless, a Harding test[3] can be utilized to evaluate business-based video items.

WCAG Guideline 2.3 Seizures and Physical Reactions give an outline not to configure the content in a way that can cause physical response or seizures. Secondly, any activity which the user can't control should not be incorporated. Thirdly, try not to structure with designs known to cause problems. Finally, if a gif or png with flashing has to be incorporated, then it should be recorded in a video group and provide options to the client to turn it off, or render it less unsafe [14].

[15] argued that the auditory descriptions for the mental model and different types of inferences are what the blind or low vision centers focus on. The study proposes to research the subject inside and out, particularly on the different methods of correspondence in cognizance and creation forms.

The study by [16] shows that multimedia resources ought to be available by giving other options, such as captions, sound, and transcripts. It reasons that all assets must be available in all their proportions to reach the critical number of users.

[17] expressed that more than 66 million individuals suffer hearing impedance, which makes it testing to comprehend video content, which includes the loss of sound data. The study suggests captioning videos helps to comprehend the content. The study recommends improving availability in videos through a dynamic captioning approach.

In 2011, [18] suggested a story that plays as the video plays and addition that involves pausing the film as long as the sound is replicated.

[19] propose exploring the most effective approach to increase the accessibility of video recordings on the web for visually impaired and low vision users in 2018, as well as implementing WCAG 2.0 for the enhancement of video generations. The experiment argues for the possibility of changing user gestures in order to better satisfy the needs of users for clear assignments.

In 2019, [20] intend to utilize WCAG 2.0 for educational purposes, as per the Web Accessibility Initiative(WAI). The research breaks down the availability of learning resources for older seniors and proposes applying new strategies to help to produce exhaustive and without any problem open assets.

A study by [21] proposes applying a consolidated technique between the programmed apparatus for photosensitive epilepsy and manual assessment with the Website Accessibility Conformance Evaluation Methodology 1.0. The study applied this strategy to 10 video assets of Latin American universities to find the lapses in video accessibility.

Subsequently, the current study suggests applying WCAG 2.1 for multimedia assets, principally for recordings, to have a huge effect on the definitive accessibility of the university's multimedia asset.

3   Methods and Material

3.1   Sample Selection

The placement of universities plays an important role in the educational setup. Despite the fact that many other positions exist for varied reasons, webometrics university assessment

---

[3] Http://www.hardingtest.com/index.php?page=test.

is the most common arrangement among higher educational institutions. The main goal of webometrics is to improve logical and social trade while also promoting open access activities.

Webometrics characterized the university sites dependent on the weightage: 50% for web content, 35% of total cited papers, 10% top referred scientists, and 5% open information share. Webometrics positioned 63 universities present in Ireland.

3.2 Units

The units used in the current study are:

- Luminance Flash: Luminance is a luminous intensity per unit area of light traveling in the given direction. It is the amount of light that passes through, is emitted from, or is reflected from a particular area and falls within a given solid angle.
- Red Flash: Any pair of opposing transitions involving a saturated red is referred to as red flash.
- Warnings: A cautionary note to examine the frames for accessibility.

3.3 Sample Size Estimation

Prior to the evaluation of the Irish university websites, the sample size was calculated. As the information is heterogeneous and the size of the domain was known, the following equation was utilized to calculate the sample size (n). [22]

$$n = \frac{N \times Z^2 \times p \times q}{d^2 \times (N - 1) + Z^2 \times p \times q}$$

where N = Population size (63); Z = level of confidence (95%), p = probability of success (50%), q = probability of failure (50%) and d = number of error proportion allowed (5%). This value was calculated with the Netquest[4] online calculator

The equation evaluation demonstrated that the sample size (n) ought to be 7. Be that as it may, for the present investigation, twofold the evaluated test size (7 x 2 = 14) is utilized to cover more universities. In this examination, 14 universities were chosen dependent on the ranking by webometrics as shown in Table 1.

3.4 Tools Selection

For the most part, the assessment of flashing or flickering in video content is assessed through automated tools. The W3C gives the technical formula to ascertain the red flash and general flickering limit. Also, the W3C suggests PEAT to check the video content instigates seizures or not.

PEAT, a free downloadable asset to assess the seizure ascends in the web content and software. Moreover, the PEAT assesses video which contains flashing or rapid transition among light and dull background hues. In the present investigation, PEAT was utilized to break down the recordings of the essential examinations.

---

[4] https://www.netquest.com/es/panel/calculadora-muestras/calculadoras-estadisticas.

Table 1. List of Universities sampled.

Ranking	World ranking	University	Acronym
1	224	Trinity College Dublin	TCD
2	252	University College Dublin	UCD
3	367	University College Cork	UCC
4	503	National University of Ireland NUI Galway	NUI
5	620	Dublin City University	DCU
6	624	University of Limerick	UL
7	1891	Maynooth University	MU
8	2040	Royal College of Surgeons of Ireland	RCSI
9	2211	Waterford Institute of Technology	WIT
10	2265	Cork Institute of Technology	CIT
11	2291	Dublin Institute For Advanced Studies	DIAS
12	3170	Galway Mayo Institute of Technology	GMIT
13	3371	Dundalk Institute of Technology	DKIT
14	3512	National College of Ireland	NCI

Figure 1 shows a screen capture of certain pictures that can upset individuals with epilepsy. The current study watches the qualities in the timecode identified with the splendor of the pictures.

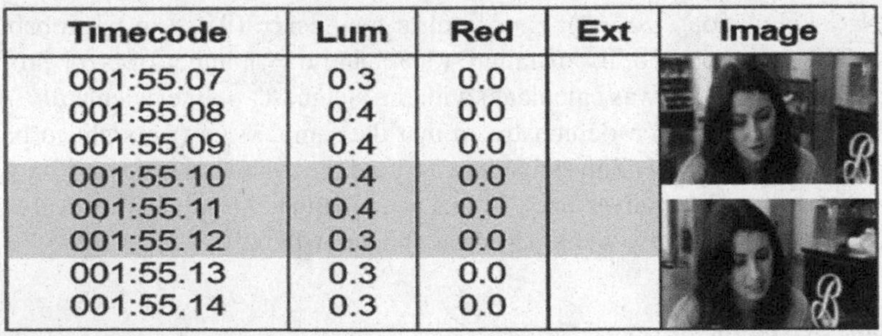

Timecode	Lum	Red	Ext	Image
001:55.07	0.3	0.0		
001:55.08	0.4	0.0		
001:55.09	0.4	0.0		
001:55.10	0.4	0.0		
001:55.11	0.4	0.0		
001:55.12	0.3	0.0		
001:55.13	0.3	0.0		
001:55.14	0.3	0.0		

Fig. 1. Frames that can change users who experience the ill effects of epilepsy

3.5 Metrics Used

The following metrics were used for the current study (Fig. 2).

- Luminance Flash: Luminance is a luminous intensity per unit area of light traveling in the given direction. It is the amount of light that passes through, is emitted from, or is reflected from a particular area and falls within a given solid angle.

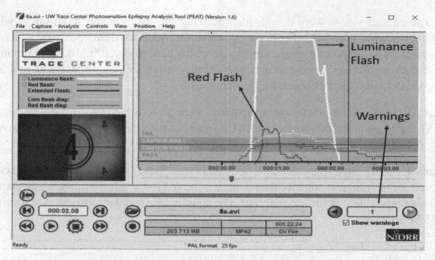

Fig. 2. Screenshot of metrics analyzed with PEAT

- Red Flash: Any pair of opposing transitions involving a saturated red is referred to as red flash.
- Warnings: A cautionary note to examine the frames for accessibility.

3.6 Method Adopted

Figure 1 shows the flowchart of the method applied to the video evaluation process. The process is summarized as follows:

Phase 1: The sample size was resolved utilizing the mathematical equation. The rundown of universities was gotten from webometrics. There were 63 enlisted universities in webometrics as per January 2020 version. The videos from the top 14 universities were chosen as primary studies as shown in Table 1.

Phase 2: On YouTube, chosen university videos were searched. For every university, three videos were haphazardly chosen. While inferring, the following incorporation standards and prohibition models were applied:

Incorporation Criteria.

- Video ought to be posted by the universities
- Video ought to be seen in any event by at least 100 viewers

Prohibition Criteria.

- Video posted other than the organizations
- Lecture and discussion recordings were discarded

The chosen videos were downloaded utilizing the BlueConvert tool(plug-in with Google Chrome) as an MP4 file. In the event that the video has numerous pixel goals, at that point most noteworthy goals, are chosen which have under 100 MB. At that point, the downloaded video is changed over to AVI video using an online conversion tool. At last, 43 AVI videos were chosen for primary studies.

Phase 3: In this phase, the following activities were performed: 1) AVI video was set on PEAT; 2) the parameters were set in PEAT; 3) photosensitive examination was employed and, 4) the results are recorded in a spreadsheet.

Phase 4: Descriptive analysis was conducted in this phase. The average value was calculated for warnings, luminance flash failures, and red flash failures for each university. The average value was further analyzed. The significance test was also calculated using IBM SPSS 25.0.

4   Result

4.1   Number of Success/Failure

Among 14 universities, only one university achieve passed above 50%. Seven universities failed in all samples. The remaining six universities achieve success below 50% as shown in Fig. 3.

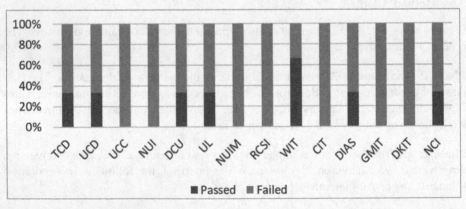

Fig. 3. Number of Success and Failures of the examined samples

4.2   Warnings

The warning is a notification or an exhortation that can hurt the epilepsy patients while seeing the recordings. On examination of exploratory information found that 50% of the warning is gotten by the recordings extracted from four universities. By and large, six universities got under 5 warmings and four universities got over 10 admonitions as shown in Fig. 4.

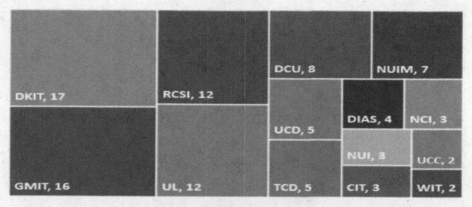

Fig. 4. Tree map view of warnings obtained for the samples

4.3 Luminance Flash Failures

Luminance flash failures were determined by the number of frames influenced by the luminance flash. The examination found that seventy-eight percent of the universities get below 100 frames of luminance streak failures. Notwithstanding, only one university peak the failure, and the remaining two universities moderate in receiving the luminance frame failure as shown in Fig. 5.

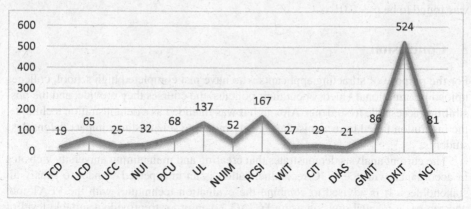

Fig. 5. Luminance Flash Failures for the examined samples

4.4 Red Flash Failures

On average, sixty-four percent of the universities receive success in achieving zero red flash frames. The research also found that twenty-one percent of the university videos have less than four red flash frames and four percent of the university videos achieve more than ten red flash failures as shown in Fig. 6.

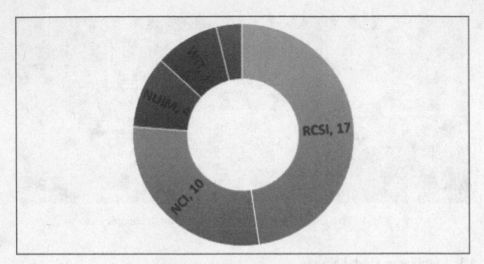

Fig. 6. Sunburst snapshot of the red flash failures

4.5 Significance Test

Linear regression was run to predict warnings, luminance flash failures, and red flash failures from the length of videos. The statistical analysis found that no significance exists to predict these variables from the duration of the videos. The significance rate was found to be $p > 0.01$.

5 Conclusion

For the purpose of attracting applicants who have just completed high school, colleges upload informational videos about their policies, the courses they provide, and the possibilities accessible to students. Although it was intended as a demonstration technique, the institution failed to recognise how easily inducing seizures may impact defenseless students.

The current analysis demonstrates that creating and maintaining university websites in accordance with the W3C recommendation is an unexpected wonder to satisfy all stakeholders. It is advised to combine the evaluation techniques with the PEAT tool and request a manual revision using WCAG 2.1 in order to provide a suitable level of multimedia assets and to create thorough recordings.

The problem of flashing videos is not simply related to university accessibility policy; it may also be managed through user browser windows. The user's browser settings may be used to change the desktop color scheme, adjust the monitor display, and block undesirable flashes. However, the user needed the knowledge to make the modifications.

This study can serve as a preliminary basis for future work related to the accessibility of multimedia resources. Moreover, the recent study will help ensure that PwE get equal chances and are not discriminated against. Finally, the current study promotes the inclusion of alternatives to enhance accessibility in multimedia resources, such as the use of dynamic captions, language settings, font size settings, colour, glow, dynamic self-description, narratives, and speed regulators in audio and video, as well as sign language.

References

1. Thijs, R.D., Surges, R., O'Brien, T.J., Sander, J.W.: Epilepsy in adults. Lancet **393**(10172), 689–701 (2019)
2. WHO: "Epilepsy", 20 June 2019. https://www.who.int/news-room/fact-sheets/detail/epilepsy. Accessed 25 May 2020
3. EpilepsyIreland, Annual Report 2017, 31 December 2017. https://www.epilepsy.ie/sites/www.epilepsy.ie/files/Annual%20Report%20-%202017_0.pdf. Accessed 25 May 2020
4. Kurt, S.: Moving toward a universally accessible web: web accessibility and education. Assistive Technol. **31**, 1–11 (2017)
5. WebAIM, Seizure Disorders, 24 March 2017. https://webaim.org/articles/scizure/. Accessed 25 May 2020
6. D. Trinity College, Accessible Information Policy & Guidelines, 8 October 2019. https://www.tcd.ie/about/policies/accessible-info-policy.php.
7. Dick,W., Jewett, T., Eggert, E., Allan, J., Benbadis, S. R.: Web accessibility for seizures and physical reactions, 19 March 2020. https://developer.mozilla.org/en-US/docs/Web/Accessibility/Seizure_disorders. Accessed 25 May 2020
8. Wirrell,E., Hernandez, A.: Photosensitivity and Seizures, 30 September 2019. https://www.epilepsy.com/learn/triggers-seizures/photosensitivity-and-seizures
9. NASA, BLINKING, FLASHING, AND TEMPORAL RESPONSE (2020). https://colorusage.arc.nasa.gov/flashing.php.
10. Harding, G., Wilkins, A.J., Erba, G., Barkley, G.L., Fisher, R.S.: Photic- and pattern-induced seizures: expert consensus of the epilepsy foundation of America working group. Epilepsia **46**(9), 1423–1425 (2005)
11. WCAG, WCAG 2.3.1 general flash and red flash thresholds (2020). https://www.w3.org/WAI/WCAG21/Understanding/three-flashes-or-below-threshold.html
12. UMD, Photosensitive Epilepsy Analysis Tool (2020). https://trace.umd.edu/peat
13. PBS, The Photosensitive Epilepsy Analysis Tool, 28 April 2010. https://www.pbs.org/video/university-place-the-photosensitive-epilepsy-analysis-tool-ep-429/
14. WCAG, WCAG Guideline 2.3 Seizures and Physical Reactions (2020). https://www.w3.org/WAI/standards-guidelines/wcag/new-in-21/
15. Braun,S.: Audio description from a discourse perspective: a socially relevant framework for research and training. Linguist. Antverp. New Ser. Transl. Stud. **6** (2007)
16. Moreno, L., Martínez, P., Ruiz-Mezcua, B.: Disability standards for multimedia on the web. IEEE Multimedia **15**(4), 52–54 (2008)
17. Hong, R., Wang, M., Yuan, X.-T., Xu, M., Jiang, J.: Video accessibility enhancement for hearing-impaired users. ACM Trans. Multimed. Comput. Commun. Appl. **7**(1), 24 (2011)
18. Szarkowska, A.: Text-to-speech audio description: towards wider. J. Specialised Transl. **15**, 142–160 (2011)
19. Funes,M.M., Trojahn, T.H., Fortes, R.P.P.M., Goularte, R.: Gesture4All: a framework for 3D gestural interaction to improve accessibility of Web videos. In: Proceedings of SAC 2018: Symposium on Applied Computing, Pau (2018)
20. Acosta-Vargas, P., et al.: Educational resources accessible on the tele-rehabilitation platform. In: Nunes, Isabel L. (ed.) AHFE 2018. AISC, vol. 781, pp. 210–220. Springer, Cham (2019). https://doi.org/10.1007/978-3-319-94334-3_22

21. Acosta-Vargas,P., Salvador-Ullauri, L., Luis Pérez-Medina, J., Rybarczyk, Y.: Accessibility evaluation of multimedia resources in selected latin america universities. In: Sixth International Conference on eDemocracy & eGovernment (ICEDEG) (2019)
22. Jarman, K.: The Art of Data Analysis: How to Answer Almost Any Question Using Basic Statistics. Wiley, Hoboken (2013)

Author Index

Printed in the United States
by Baker & Taylor Publisher Services